Praise for *Teaching Twos and Threes*

"Although this book is full of wonderful activities for twos and threes, it goes far beyond a typical activity book by allowing teachers to follow the child's lead and design a curriculum based on the natural behaviors and curiosities of this unique age group. This is the type of book that will support teachers who want to grow along with twos and threes. It's a fresh resource that encourages a reflective creative practice."

**Carol Garboden Murray, director of the Bard College
Nursery School, NYSAEYC-credentialed early learning trainer,
and author of *Simple Signing with Young Children***

"*Teaching Twos and Threes* goes above and beyond providing a curriculum. Deborah offers specific and authentic—and, most of all, respectful—advice that fully captures the delight in experiencing this extraordinary age group. Her creative strategies present inspired, individualized ideas for helping nurture children as they grow into confident problem solvers. As a caregiver of two-year-olds, I immediately began applying the ideas found in this book to my own classroom on the very same day that I read it! Deborah is truly an expert in her field, and *Teaching Twos and Threes* would make a perfect textbook or refresher course for new and veteran educators alike."

**Kelly Zechmeister-Smith, MEd, North Campus
Children's Center, University of Michigan**

"Deborah Falasco's to-the-point, easy-reading curriculum planning book for twos and threes will be very helpful to educators and child care providers who may wonder or have been struggling with how to create a comprehensive curriculum for young children. It promotes a variety of ways to support children's learning while they are playing. Unlike other curriculum books, Falasco supports her curriculum ideas with information on child development as well as the benefits of the curriculum and learning areas. It is a must-have book for educators and child care providers of young children."

**Ayuko Uezu Boomer, MSEd, early childhood specialist, Shirley G. Moore
Laboratory School, University of Minnesota**

Teaching Twos and Threes

Teaching Twos and Threes

A COMPREHENSIVE CURRICULUM

Deborah Falasco

Redleaf Press®
www.redleafpress.org
800-423-8309

Published by Redleaf Press
10 Yorkton Court
St. Paul, MN 55117
www.redleafpress.org

First edition 2014
Cover design by Jim Handrigan
Cover photograph by Deborah Falasco
Interior design by Percolator
Typeset in Apex and Cassia
Interior photographs by Deborah Falasco
Printed in the United States of America
20 19 18 17 16 15 14 13   1 2 3 4 5 6 7 8

Library of Congress Cataloging-in-Publication Data
Falasco, Deborah.
  Teaching twos and threes : a comprehensive curriculum / Deborah Falasco.
      pages cm
   Includes index.
   Summary: "With a focus on the special joys of working with two- and three-year-olds,
this comprehensive curriculum meets the unique developmental needs of this age group
and supports critical early learning. *Teaching Twos and Threes* includes a wide range of
activity ideas and learning experiences, as well as strategies to help you plan a thoughtful
program, build positive relationships with young children, and support learning in all
areas" — Provided by publisher.
   ISBN 978-1-60554-132-7 (pbk.)
   ISBN 978-1-60554-257-7 (e-book)
   1. Early childhood education—Curricula—United States. 2. Early childhood education—
Activity programs—United States. 3. Child development—United States.   I. Title.
   LB1139.4.F35 2013
   372.71—dc23
                          2013004538

Printed on acid-free paper

To Jennifer, Brian, and Katrina—
my forever inspiration

Contents

Acknowledgments

I would like to thank the following people: my parents (who gave me my foundation), my children (who taught me the most about children), my husband (who dealt with my many hours of college studies and book writing), my siblings, and the friends who supported and encouraged me to aspire to be more and step further—believing in me. To the many children who have shared the journeys and adventures with me (from my family child care days to my current nook at Vassar) and *all* of my *amazing* models who brought this book to life—thank you! May all children feel the love and respect of their adults, and spend their days with a smile and a warm heart!

Introduction

I began my career in family child care. I loved the small group, the cozy environment, and the intimate relationships I developed with families. I will forever cherish those memories.

Toward the end of my family child care days, I began to pursue my formal training as an educator. I felt that I had a great deal of experience, but I needed to combine my practical skills with a better understanding of education to best serve children and their families.

Eventually I closed my family child care and went to work at a preschool for children with special needs. I loved that experience as well, and I enjoyed learning from the master teachers there.

I then found my way to the laboratory nursery school on the campus of Vassar College. This school was very different from my first two early childhood environments. A laboratory school is a teaching and learning environment for both children and adults. Each classroom has an observation booth to help student educators and their professors discreetly observe the children, teachers, and classroom environment. I remember my first day in the booth, watching the two-year-olds and feeling at home. I had a passion for this age group.

I earned my bachelor's degree in early education. I then decided to get my master's degree, focusing on the zero-to-three age group. I felt this was a special age in children's development, and I valued the integral role families play in the lives of children three and younger. I searched for very particular degree programs. I earned a graduate certification as an infant-toddler specialist. After that, I pursued my master's degree in human development, specializing in infants, toddlers, and their families. By this time, I was teaching in a classroom of two- and three-year-olds. My day job helped me practice what I was learning, and my master's program helped me question and reflect on my teaching practice.

Eleven-plus years later, I've loved every moment I've spent with two- and three-year-olds. Becoming an infant-toddler specialist and mentoring others has been very gratifying for me. I delight in working closely with children's families while teaching and loving their children. Two- and three-year-olds are very busy, curious, lovable, and fun. I cannot imagine an age I would rather work with!

My profession is my passion. I want to share my experiences in and ideas on teaching twos and threes with as many teachers as I can. I've written this book to help you become mindful of this age group's needs in planning your curriculum. I also want to help you become reflective about your teaching practice.

Creating a balanced program for twos and threes is no easy task. Society places many academic expectations on preschoolers and prekindergarteners, and these expectations often reach down to even younger children. Children between two and three years old are no longer babies or young toddlers—and yet they are not preschoolers either. I have taught this age group for many years, and the growth between the second and third year still amazes me. This book is intended to help teachers see two- and three-year-olds as they are, developmentally speaking, and to help teachers create developmentally appropriate programs that are stimulating and authentic for *all* twos and threes.

In the past, I have offered workshops geared toward teachers and caregivers of older toddlers (eighteen months and older) and two-year-olds. I began by asking the participants where they saw their biggest challenges and their best delights. Almost all the educators mentioned difficulty with young children's impulse control, short attention spans, toileting, varying ability levels, pushing, hitting, biting, and testing limits. The participants enjoyed the wonder in working with the under-three population. The activities they noted as enjoyable were singing and dancing, hands-on art, and watching new experiences.

We all have felt the occasional struggle and exhaustion of working with this age group. Fortunately, even more often we feel the delight of working with twos and threes. We get the honor and pleasure of being an important helper at a crucial moment in a child's life—the developmental leap into independence. How we touch the lives of our students and families in this moment leaves permanent footprints.

All about This Marvelous Age Group

Working with two- and three-year-olds is a lively experience. Twos and threes are sweet and feisty all at once. They are tender, warm, and loving. They are bursting with giggles and mischief. Everything is new and exciting to them. They look at the world with wonder and anticipation. Throughout their days, they are constantly finding out how things work and what happens next.

Twos and threes are in a delicate state. They are not babies or young toddlers. At twenty-four through forty-two months old, they are leaving toddlerhood and becoming preschoolers. They are gaining independence and learning about themselves and their place in the world around them. Their egocentrism is transforming into awareness. They are developing important relationship skills, such as empathy and the give-and-take of relationships, often through trial and error. Twos and threes have different emotional, intellectual, and physical needs than preschoolers have.

WHY DO TWOS AND THREES NEED AN ENVIRONMENT DIFFERENT FROM A PRESCHOOL?

Twos and threes are finding their way through the world as people separate from their families—among other children navigating similar developmental challenges. Achieving autonomy is hard work! Twos and threes need adult support and a warm and nurturing environment to help them do this work. In addition, they may be at different stages in their development. For example, many twos and threes may still mouth materials. They need materials thoughtfully designed for children ages twenty-four to forty-two months. Finally, two- and three-year-olds have much shorter attention spans than preschoolers have. Teachers must consider this reality when planning all aspects of the curriculum.

WHY DO TWOS AND THREES NEED A STIMULATING CURRICULUM?

For twos and threes, a stimulating curriculum is the doorway to a lifelong love of learning. A stimulating environment keeps their hands and bodies busy while their brains are making magnificent connections. And on the flip side: a program that is not stimulating leads to boredom, aggression, and tears!

WHAT CONSTITUTES A STIMULATING CURRICULUM FOR TWOS AND THREES?

Twos and threes need you to be a facilitator, a loving caretaker, and a partner in learning. They need you to plan a curriculum that balances safety and free exploration. Offer many opportunities for children to really experience and experiment with materials. Twos and threes need hands-on, sensory experiences to help them clearly understand new ideas and skills. They also need repetition, repetition, repetition! That is how they learn. Coming back to previous learning and then building onto it is key to mastery for this age group. You must introduce new concepts and skills in concrete ways that show value in their world in order to catch their interest.

HOW CAN WE HELP TWOS AND THREES BECOME INDEPENDENT?

We want young children to be inquisitive about their world. When we pique their curiosity and give them some freedom, we help them become motivated learners and keen problem solvers for a lifetime. The layout of your environment is key to fostering independence. First, make sure the classroom equipment is safe and appropriate for children of this age range (twenty-four to forty-two months). Twos and threes tend to run and climb more than preschoolers do, so you must plan for this. Second, when you design the environment and curriculum, create opportunities for success and independence. See that tasks and activities are developmentally appropriate so children can master them over time. Observe what works and what does not.

How to Get Started

How do we begin to develop, or add more depth to, our teaching practice as we work with two- and three-year-olds? As we recognize the importance of this amazing year in children's lives, how do we tailor our programs to suit the unique needs of this age group?

First we need to get to know the children within the group. We need to begin developing relationships with them—and with their families. We need to observe the children carefully and then begin to lay the foundation for the year by building a curriculum fit just to them. *Teaching Twos and Threes* carefully addresses program curriculum areas appropriate to children in this age group.

When I was a new teacher, I found myself focusing on improving one curriculum area at a time, beginning with those I felt were weakest in my teaching practice. All along, I sought to find new ideas, and I tried various techniques to see what worked well and what did not. And as I recorded my ideas and suggestions in this book, I kept in mind that what works well differs for each of us, as does what works best for each program, as well as for each child. It is my hope that this book will be helpful and inspiring to teachers and caregivers of all experience levels.

Chapters 1 and 2 of *Teaching Twos and Threes* aim to offer you a starting point for developing the ideas presented—or for developing new ideas. They offer a place to begin reflecting on—or to continue reflecting on—your teaching practice. They are designed to inspire you to think deeply about observation and about getting to know the children, as well as to understand and define the how, the what, and the why of curriculum planning for this age group. They suggest ideas for brainstorming and a different perspective on how to understand and tackle challenging behaviors and situations not uncommon to a twos-and-threes classroom. When teachers and caregivers strive to find positive solutions to challenges, as you know, they create their own learning moments and personal development opportunities.

The rest of the chapters in the book offer ideas and activities organized by areas that are familiar to all twos-and-threes classrooms—for example, art, circle time, and dramatic play. (There are chapters on science and nature, cooking, and writing exploration too!) These chapters can be read in any order you desire. The appendixes offer a variety of helpful planning information (you'll find a curriculum planning template in appendix A), as well as recipes and song lyrics.

Each early childhood educator who has the pleasure and honor to work with children in this spectacular age group has a truly important job to do, one that will impact children in the earliest stages of their learning. I hope you are able to take great delight in your work with twos and threes. I want to thank you for all that you do. Now let's begin!

CHAPTER 1

Curriculum Planning, Observation, Recording, and Evaluation

Planning a curriculum for two- and three-year-olds is a delicate balancing act. This age group needs a more advanced curriculum than infants and toddlers do. But it cannot be too complex—nor can it be a watered-down preschool program. The activities need to be inviting and stimulating for this specific age group.

Teachers need to be observant. You must really *know* your children, both as a group and as individuals. Be aware that what works one year with one group may not work the next year for another group. It's essential to tailor your curriculum to each particular group of children.

Flexibility is key. You may start with an excellent plan, but your children may have another excellent plan in mind! You need to follow their lead to see how things go. Be able to switch gears and do things differently if necessary.

Curriculum Planning

As you begin to plan, it is important to think about safety and logistics, and to develop relationships with children first. Purposeful planning unfolds as you begin to get a good understanding of the group of children you have, their needs, and their likes. Designing thoughtful and mindful planning takes time, but it is well worth the effort.

BEING MINDFUL AND PURPOSEFUL

To plan a high-quality curriculum, you must be mindful and purposeful. You need to ask yourself continuously, "Why do I want to teach this? What do I want the children to learn or gain?" Design a curriculum that not only makes progress toward your goals for the children but also works well for you personally and for the children individually and collectively.

As you plan a curriculum for two- and three-year-olds, consider the following:

- What is relevant to the children? Consider who is in their world, what they see and do, and possible useful and fun things to learn.

- How can you build respectful relationships? At this age, children and their families are a package deal. Families deserve recognition and respect for their important role, and a sense of partnership between home and school is very important. Attachment and respect between the children and adults are important too. Each teacher-child relationship must develop individually. Finally, children need to form healthy relationships with other children. The children in your program will be exploring their school, community, and world together, learning and growing along the way.

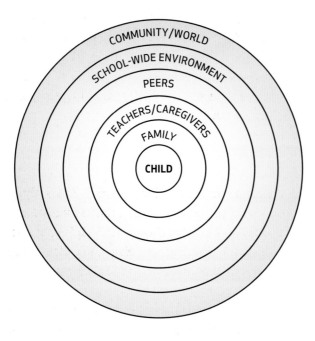

THINKING ABOUT THE WHOLE YEAR

Before you try to plan your daily curriculum, you might want to think about the year as a whole. You could begin the year with units woven of learning foundations, such as building relationships and self-help skills. These units have a specific purpose and meaning beyond exposure to the subject matter. They function as typical theme-based units, which many schools require. But they serve a deeper purpose too.

For example, a unit on babies at the beginning of the year introduces the concepts of empathy and caring for another person. A subsequent unit on "me as a baby" adds perspective. It helps children think about how they were once little, that somebody used to care tenderly for them as well, and

that they are bigger and more capable now. This leads into a unit on pets, which provides another way to think about care, respect, and capability.

In a similar way, a unit on construction goes deeper than learning about trucks and tools. It offers children a chance to learn about what happens in a construction zone (what the trucks are, what the tools are, and who the workers are) and then to apply their learning with hands-on simulation in the classroom. This unit helps children start to think of themselves as workers, a concept that continues to develop throughout the year. In this unit and subsequent ones, the workers are encouraged to identify goals and develop a plan they can carry out to reach each goal. As they carry out their plans, they learn to follow a sequence, help one another, and be mindful. Trial and error in both making a plan and executing it are crucial to this learning.

Food units offer opportunities to explore many learning objectives. Your food units might begin with an introduction to nutrition, developing good eating habits, and making healthy food choices. You could further explore food with units on restaurants, bakeries, grocery stores, harvesting apples or pumpkins, or gardening. Within these units you can teach children about roles and responsibilities, table manners, cooking and preparing meals, working together as a group, following directions, counting, sorting, classifying, buying, and selling. Such units can help children understand where food comes from, why it's important to eat healthfully, and how to be a member of a group during meals. Many skills introduced through food units become valuable thereafter in everyday experiences.

Literacy units work well in the middle of the school year. You might begin with discussing how stories can have various versions (different variations, interpretations, or readings). Without using those terms, you can convey their meaning through demonstration. For example, you could read "Goldilocks and the Three Bears" once using a gentle "Papa Bear" voice and again using a grouchy "Papa Bear" voice. Or you could read "The Three Little Pigs" first using a sweet "Wolfie" voice and then using a loud "Big Bad Wolf" voice. Such reading creates a wonderful opportunity to work through the story and any fears it might arouse in children. It also offers an opportunity to discuss real and pretend ideas, right and wrong, and good and bad characters.

Next, you can introduce the concept that a story can be told in many different ways. For example, you might bring a story to life by reading a book aloud, playing a recording, singing a song, or dramatizing the story with a felt board, finger puppets, shadow puppets, masks, or props.

A tray showing various storytelling props

Literacy units like these help children develop a love of reading and an appreciation for stories and storytelling. Such units also introduce the notion that we are all storytellers—each child and adult. Each of us can be an author and an illustrator by expressing our thoughts through words and through drawings at our writing tables.

You can enrich and expand your literacy units with rhymes. You could spend an entire month or more teaching one or two rhymes a day. Each day, pose the question: "What is a nursery rhyme?" Before long, the children will know how to respond: "It's a short story . . . that rhymes!" You could then play a game of thinking about rhyming words. Give the children an example, such as, "*House* rhymes with *mouse*!" Then invite the children to say their own examples. Present nursery rhymes, poems, and songs in a way that invites the children into the stories and offers them opportunities to explore

and internalize each rhyme. You will see evidence of their understanding of the rhymes in their play and work. A great way for children to finish a unit is by acting out rhymes they've learned. Rhyming is a wonderful way to build early literacy. It is exciting to hear children learn and recite rhymes, songs, and poems while they increase their vocabulary, discrimination of sounds, comprehension, and memory skills.

Rounding out the school year, spring and summer lend themselves well to units about the natural world and how we fit into it. Learning to be mindful of nature builds understanding, respect, connection, and love for the natural world. Nature units might include the topics of spring, gardening, butterflies, insects, birds, frogs, pond life, rain, dirt, mud, water, and more.

BEING FLEXIBLE

Planning a curriculum for twos and threes differs from year to year, depending on the individual children who make up the classroom. Careful observation of each individual, as well as the entire group, will help you determine your initial curriculum design.

Teachers should begin the year with a loose plan. In the early days, an optimal plan is one that can be tweaked as necessary. A simple plan using popular topics and materials is best.

With this age group, much of the curriculum involves routines. Meals, diapering, toileting, resting, separations, peer interactions, social skills, and self-help skills are all important activities that make up a day. Other activities are almost secondary. Responsive caregiving fosters relationships and aids in responsive planning.

After setting a loose plan in motion, the teacher should watch how the children respond to it. The teacher can assess the children's responses to figure out whether changes are in order. This process should repeat itself many times. Planning, observation, evaluation, and more planning should form a continuous, cyclical process that lasts throughout the year.

As teachers of twos and threes, we must follow our students' lead in planning the curriculum. We need to be consistent yet flexible. We need to change things when changes are clearly necessary. Sometimes children aren't as interested as we thought they would be. Sometimes an unexpected problem or an unforeseen new idea pops up! Expect the unexpected. And be prepared just to go with it. Such flexibility often leads to beautiful teachable moments. Remember that even if your curriculum veers off course, if it is child driven, it's still valuable.

If you find yourself beginning to say no as a child makes a risky choice—or simply takes a different direction than you had planned—stop and quickly question yourself: "Why say no? And for that matter, why say yes?" If you allow something another teacher might not allow, what is your reason? What is the lesson, knowledge, or experience the child will gain? Sometimes there is a fine line between breaking rules and learning. Knowing when to say yes and when to say no to a risky investigation takes flexible thinking, respect, and trust between child and adult.

· ·

It was the third week of a construction unit. The children were really enjoying the unit, inside the classroom and outdoors, through many planned and unplanned construction activities. The first week had focused on construction vehicles. The second week had focused on tools. The third week focused on the workers and their roles, offering sample worker experiences to the children.

One child took this role play to heart. Justin exuded the worker persona 100 percent. Sometimes he was the foreman who took calls and sent the proper workers for jobs that needed doing. In one case, Justin wanted to do the job himself. He donned a hard hat and tool belt. He took apart the sink in the dramatic play area and began climbing inside the cabinet.

The typical adult response would be to quickly say, "Feet on the floor," or "We don't climb on furniture," or a similar message. As other adults in the room jumped to curb Justin's risky behavior, the teacher told them to wait.

She asked him, "What's your plan? What are you thinking about?"

Justin answered, "I gotta fix the sink."

The teacher, curious about his thought process and what he might do next, said, "Oh, I see. So how will you do that? Tell me your plan."

A "worker" repairs the sink.

Ask the child, "What's your plan?"

As Justin continued dismantling the furniture, he explained his plan thoughtfully, "Well, I need to take this [sink top] off and climb in." He began to climb inside. He made several attempts. Each time he tried to climb inside, the furniture pieces separated, and he dropped the tools in his hands.

"How about a chair to help you climb?" the teacher offered.

"Yes, I need that!" Justin replied.

He threw the tools into the sink and ran to get a small chair. The teacher helped him line up the chair carefully for safety. He climbed into the sink and continued his work, complete with lots of screeches from his drill and pounding from his hammer.

What did Justin learn from this experience? He assumed the role of a worker. He saw a problem—a broken sink—and decided to fix it. But how? He formed a plan. He had to climb inside and work on it. But how could he do that? The teacher supported him and helped keep him safe. He saw that she not only valued but also encouraged his ideas. This experience gave him confidence.

· ·

A curriculum plan is important because it gives you a base or a starting point. It helps you provide a well-thought-out program that suits your group of young children both developmentally and temperamentally. Your plan can change based on the needs, moods, and interests of the children.

Many books offer ideas on planning the curriculum for two- and three-year-olds. In my early teaching days, I relied mainly on three early childhood curriculum systems: Creative Curriculum, Innovations, and HighScope. All of them offered a wide array of ideas, advice, and information for setting up a solid twos-and-threes program. I compared the three systems for a class I was taking at the time, and I found that I really enjoyed many aspects of each. I recommend learning about a few styles of curricula to see what works best for you personally and for the center where you teach.

A WRITTEN DAILY PLAN

A written daily curriculum plan gives you a tool to plan age-appropriate activities for your children every day. It will help keep your daily activities on track and can provide a starting point for reflection when the time comes. A written daily plan also

- provides an overall idea of what you are doing with the children;

- provides a vehicle for thematic planning, if needed;

- helps you ensure that your program meets the children's needs; and

- helps you see patterns of interest in this particular group of children.

As we teachers become more experienced in the classroom, we begin to see what works best for each of us individually in regard to daily curriculum planning. We begin to develop a written planning method. Some people prefer to buy a planning book that covers the whole year. Some teachers make copies from planning templates in books. Some teachers use the computer to design planning sheets tailored to their own needs and classroom routines. For example, I developed my curriculum planning sheets to reflect the way I teach, schedule daily activities, and arrange my classroom. Each of my planning sheets covers one week. (See appendix A for a template, as well as completed examples.) The reverse side provides space for personal notes to help me reflect on the week's activities and think about future tweaks.

STAFF RELATIONSHIPS AND CURRICULUM PLANNING

Staff relationships may seem tangential to curricula, but actually, they profoundly affect curriculum planning. Many teachers of twos and threes work in teams. Team teaching and classroom sharing are like marriage in some ways. Coteachers need to have good communication, flexibility, and the ability to see another person's perspective. Truthfully, sharing a classroom can be a lot of work—even with the best of relationships.

Coteachers must discuss their teaching philosophies. Ideally these philosophies should be very similar. Minimally coteachers should have the same clear expectations from children. Coteachers cannot have inconsistent rules. For example, if one teacher insists that feet are always planted securely on the floor, but a coteacher lets children climb to get materials or allows sitting on tables, the children receive contradictory messages. This is confusing for the children, who will never be sure what's acceptable behavior. They might even play one adult against the other, as children sometimes do with parents.

Working alongside people with whom you share a teaching philosophy is wonderful. But even with a highly compatible teaching team, concerns and disagreements will arise. Open communication is the best policy at all times. Coteachers must discuss philosophical differences and strong feelings about any issue or topic. They must show respect toward one another—in front of children and families, as well as in private.

In a less-compatible teaching team, differences are more likely. Use differences as opportunities for personal growth. You will learn some very important things about yourself if you are open to new ideas and willing to be reflective and honest. You will learn what is of high value to you. You will discover where you can compromise and where you simply cannot. Every teacher has something she can teach another, and even the most skilled and experienced teacher can always learn something from another person.

If coteachers' philosophies are extremely different, the discord could make planning very difficult. When working with someone becomes too difficult, it is best to go to your director and ask for help in solving the problem productively and respectfully.

PLANNING FOR SMOOTH ENTRIES

A strategically planned curriculum will help children make smooth entries into your program. A well-arranged schedule helps new children know what to expect each day. And a specific plan for new students can ease the transition for them.

Some programs have time built into their schedule at the beginning of the year for classroom setup, home visits by teachers, and gradual entry by children. Such time and flexibility are extremely helpful for children, families, and teachers alike.

I know, however, from my years in family child care that many programs do not have this luxury. In fact, many programs have no beginning or end at all. One year runs into the next, and children revolve in and out as they grow. Can you build a solid program and trusting relationships without the luxury of time? Absolutely! You know best how to adapt your program to new children and new needs.

If you can build setup time, home visits, and gradual entry into your program, it will make a world of difference. Following are some suggestions to help you plan for smooth entries.

Setup

When you have time to set up your classroom without children present, you have an opportunity to make a clean, fresh start—both literally and figuratively. You can clean and organize your space, which is beneficial to all. You can talk with other teachers, plan your curriculum, and get ready to put it in motion. Many schools use setup time as an opportunity for professional training as well.

Home Visits

Home visits offer you a wonderful opportunity to see children in their home environments. You can gain a lot of information in a short period just by observing children in their "natural habitat." You can also begin to develop trust. You can make a one-on-one connection with each child and family. Children and their families feel comfortable and safe in their own environment. When they feel secure, they are more likely to ask and answer important questions.

Gradual Entry

Gradual entry means letting new children enter your program slowly instead of starting full-time on the first day, which can be difficult for children who have never been in child care before. Some children separate from their families easily and may need little more than a hug and a kiss before jumping right in. Other children need more support. Starting child care slowly offers a child small, manageable chunks of time in which to get to know you, the other children, the environment, and the schedule; to build trust; and to experience family members leaving and returning. Gradual entry also gives you an opportunity to get to know new children and families, build trust and respect, and provide small samples of your program.

How do you create a thoughtful and gentle gradual entry? Here are some tips:

- Have a well-thought-out plan and time schedule for new children. Plan with purpose. Think about what you hope to accomplish in these early days. A few important goals are trust, respect, comfort, security, establishing routines, and building consistency.

- Run through your plan carefully in your head and on paper.

- Design your gradual entry plan to give new children a small sample of each portion of your day.

- Don't plan too many or too stimulating activities for new children.

- Plan simple activities that will engage but not overwhelm new children. Focus on light, fun activities that help you build relationships.

- During the entry period, invite family members to stay if they want to.

- If possible, split your group in half for the first one to three days and offer activities in two sessions. New children may acclimate better in smaller groups.

- For a new child's first few days, gradually increase the length of the stay. Offer typical activities in shortened periods that follow the normal sequence of your day. A gradual entry schedule might look something like this:

Day One (1.5 Hours)

9:00–9:30 free play and material exploration with assorted activities

9:30–9:40 toileting, diaper changes, hand washing

9:40–10:00 group snack

10:00–10:30 outdoor playtime

Days Two and Three (2.5 Hours)

9:00–9:45 free play and material exploration with assorted activities

9:45–9:55 toileting, diaper changes, hand washing

9:55–10:15 group snack

10:15–10:25 circle time (short, familiar song or book)

10:25–11:30 outdoor playtime

Day Four and Beyond (Full Day)

8:00–9:00 free play and material exploration with assorted activities (including indoors and outdoors)

9:00–9:15 toileting, diaper changes, hand washing

9:15–9:35 group snack

9:35–9:50 circle time (group gathering)

9:50–10:30 choice activities (centers, activities)

10:30–11:45 outdoor playtime/exploration

11:45–11:55 toileting, diaper changes, hand washing

12:00–12:25 lunch

12:25–12:35 books, settle in for rest time

12:40–2:30 individual rest time as needed for individual resting patterns

1:30–2:30 diaper changing, toileting, hand washing, quiet activities

2:30–2:45 afternoon snack (outside if weather permits)

2:45–3:30 outdoor playtime

Separation Tips

Some new children may have difficulty separating from their families during their early days in your program. To help these children, make sure your entry plan incorporates comfort items and sensible good-byes.

Comfort items might include family photos, a family member's article of clothing (such as a scarf with perfume on it), or a photo holder on a spiral keychain that a child can wear on her wrist. A child may have a favorite stuffed animal, toy, doll, blanket, sippy cup, or pacifier that could ease separation.

Make certain that each family member dropping off a new child says good-bye. Sneaking out to avoid tears is a grave mistake. It is a short-term solution that shatters trust. When family members leave without saying good-bye, children feel anxious and uncertain about when—or if—their family will return. And on following days, the children won't know when their family members might come or go, so they begin to cling to their families.

Building trust takes time. A child learns to trust a new environment through the family's consistency, honesty, and reassurance about the environment's safety and the family's return. Here are some tips for facilitating good-byes:

- Give a time frame for the family member's departure. For example: "In two minutes, Mommy needs to go to work."

- Give an activity-based time frame for departure. For example: "After two books, Daddy needs to go."

- When it's departure time, don't waffle. Follow through on the promised time frame. Be consistent, and help the family member gently say good-bye.

- Encourage the family member to let the child know exactly when he will return. For example: "I will be back after your nap" or "I will be back after your snack."

- Offer the child a comfort item. Let children keep comfort items as long as they need them, for such items are very important for some children.

- As the family member leaves, hold and comfort the child. Suggest an appealing activity right away. (You might even want to suggest it ahead of time.) These actions not only help the child, but also tell the family that you will always be there to help the child and that all will be well when they leave.

Observation, Recording, and Evaluation

Planning is just the first step toward achieving a high-quality curriculum for twos and threes. We also need to reflect on our curriculum to identify what is working and what is not. Observation and recording reveal the strengths and weaknesses in our programs. Evaluation helps us plan changes to strengthen our weak spots.

Several books offer examples and guidelines, discuss observation methods, and provide rating scales to ensure appropriate practice. The Infant/ Toddler Rating Scale is a good evaluation model to follow. It is comprehensive and will keep you thinking about important elements that are easy to forget in both your program and your practice. You can find more information for *The Infant/Toddler Environmental Rating Scale*, Revised, or *The Early Childhood Environment Rating Scale*, Revised, at http:// ers.fpg.unc.edu/about-environment-rating-scales.

OBSERVATION

Observation is critical to a good program, for it provides you with the information you need to understand each child, to build positive relationships with children and their families, and to plan the activities and environments that help children learn best.

Observation of children begins with your first meeting and continues through the first few days while you get to know the children in your care. These early observations reveal basic things, such as a child's temperament, whether separations are difficult, likes and dislikes, whether everything goes in the mouth, developmental delays, a tendency to repeat unsafe behaviors, and so on. Early observations tell us how to set our environments and early curriculum in order to keep children safe.

As time goes on, you can use observations in a variety of ways. You can observe children to learn more about their personalities, their relationships with their families and peers, their development, and their interests. You can observe children to find out what they say and do during particular time periods or activities or to study particular behaviors. These later observations can help you set goals for children, plan experiences for them, and shape your overall program.

If you are like most teachers of two- and three-year-olds, you rarely have time to step away from the action to sit and observe without other responsibilities. Things continuously happen. Diapers need to be changed. The room gets wild! Instead, observe children while you are engaged with them. For example, join children in a particular learning center or watch the children's interactions. Find ways to be in the moment with children and note what is happening.

As you practice observing in the moment with your children, it will become second nature to you. You'll do it without even thinking about it. You'll learn more than you could have guessed about children's language, emotional wellness, thoughts and ideas, intentions, interests, and much, much more.

Learning *how* to observe takes practice. You must watch and listen objectively, not subjectively.

One of my professors explained that this means being aware of your cultural lens. Like all teachers, you come to your classroom with a set of personal experiences that can color your view of what's actually happening. Leave your past and your opinions behind. Watch and listen without judgment.

RECORDING

You can choose from many types of official recording methods. Your choice depends on what information you are seeking and the circumstances surrounding it. Whatever method you choose, record just what you see and hear, not what you think the mood or intention is. Include as much factual detail as possible.

Personally, I prefer a simple method of anecdotal records or journaling. I typically carry small notepads and scrap paper in my pockets. I continuously write notes about things I see and hear. A note could be something funny a child says to share later with a family member. (Most families love getting a snapshot from their children's day.) Or a note might be a statement from a child about her play or work. When I keep records this way, I find that later, when I need to know or verify something about a child, I can easily grab a quote, an incident note, or a fact to shed light on things.

If this method sounds like a good fit for you, find ways to be in the moment with children and jot notes for later, more legible recording. Keep notepads or scrap paper handy. You can abbreviate words or write just the key words and come back later to rewrite your notes in more depth. Don't wait too long to record or rewrite your notes, as you might forget about the notes or forget the details of your observation. Taking photos along with notes may help you remember details. (For more information on photo documentation, see page 16–17.)

I record my observations in other ways too. For example, I take photos during play and activities. I save sample drawings and other artwork. I occasionally make checklists to organize particular information about the group as a whole, such as who can follow two-step directions, who can pedal a bike, and so on. Or when certain behaviors, such as biting or aggression, are becoming problematic, I may use time and event sampling to observe more carefully. Time sampling is watching for certain behaviors at set times throughout the day or over several days to look for patterns and find out what the child is doing at specific times during the school day. Event sampling is noting how often a particular behavior is happening, as well as details around each occurrence.

Good records paint a picture of each child. Your observations and notes are key to formulating the best plan of action.

EVALUATION

What do you do with all your notes, photos, and samples? Try to file them. (*Try* is the key word—it can be hard to remember.) Save your records in envelopes, folders, or boxes. As soon as possible, try to type out your full observation. You might also want to keep a journal for more subjective thoughts and reflections. Such a journal may help you reflect on your group and your practice, or you may want to share it with your teaching team when asking for advice on a particular child or situation.

Later you can analyze your observations to help you track and understand each child's growth and development, spot atypical developments, set goals for the individual children and the class, complete report cards, prepare for conferences, tweak your curriculum, and so forth. Reflection is critical. You must look deeply and give profound thought to what your observations reveal. Then use those revelations to improve your program.

As teachers, we all need to look at our programs to assess whether we are operating safely and offering a loving, nurturing program that stimulates positive growth and development for the children within our group. Even veteran teachers must always examine, adapt, and change their programs and classrooms to be sure they are providing the best care possible for the children and families within their programs.

As you analyze your observations and evaluate your program, ask yourself these hard—but important—questions:

1. *How is your program running?* Does it feel smooth or bumpy? Keeping a journal or taking notes will help you reflect on how things are going. You will begin to see patterns. If your program feels bumpy, your notes will help you detect where the problem lies and figure out how to rectify it.

2. *Where do you find the most difficulty?* Does it occur at the same time in the schedule? Are particular children involved? What can you tweak to get through those difficult moments?

3. *How are the transitions?* Poor transitions are stressful for young children. If transitions are tricky in your group, use your documentation to develop a strategy to improve them.

4. *Are the current routines comfortable for the children?* Are they age appropriate? Do they meet the children's needs? Are the children capable of meeting your expectations? Finding balance in routines takes time and careful attention. Remember that children with special needs require additional assistance and individualized plans.

5. *Does the day flow nicely or drag on endlessly?* Do ten minutes feel like one second or an hour? Your day will drag if you feel unfocused and the children are not fully engaged. Your day will flow if it's well planned. Achieving good flow often takes trial and error.

6. *Are the children engaged, or do they seem bored?* A challenging and stimulating environment will keep the children engaged. If they either seem bored or are running or moving about actively, they may need either more stimulation or activities that better suit their needs. Take careful note of when the classroom mood changes and who is involved. Try to discover whether one or two children cause the change or if it is more of a planning issue.

7. *Are there any new materials you can add?* Are the materials holding the children's interest? Are the materials the same day after day, or do you rotate materials often? Do the materials challenge the children? Can you adjust or add materials to spice up a particular area or activity?

8. *Are the activities you've chosen age appropriate, interesting, and purposeful?* Have you given thought to *why* you have planned certain activities? Use careful observation and note taking to detect and assess the effectiveness of your activities.

9. *When you correct behaviors, are your methods effective for each child in the group?* Have you planned individually for children with special needs? On the whole, are your discipline techniques effective? Do the children respond positively? If you catch yourself shouting, snapping, or constantly reprimanding, stop to evaluate why this is happening and how you can improve.

10. *How do you interact with children?* When you work with this age group, it is crucial to meet them at their level and develop respectful relationships. Do you lower your body to their level? Do you use a soft and appropriate voice? Are you patient when listening to children? Do you treat all children equally and with respect?

11. *Do your facial expressions and body language convey respect and kindness?* Are they appropriate to the messages you're speaking? Children are very intuitive; they can read more about our emotions and body language than we think they can. Once I had a little boy tell me he did not want to be on the playground with the teacher with the "boring eyes." Eventually I found out that he was referring to a teacher who, he felt, often wore an angry face. A serious message needs a serious face—but no message needs an angry face.

12. *Are you aware of the language you use both in discipline and during general conversation?* Are your messages authentic and personal or generic and flat? Each child is truly an individual and needs to be treated as such. Speaking authentically to children is easy when you really know each child within your program.

13. *Do you talk about children's art as "pretty" and "beautiful"?* If necessary, adapt your language to get rid of meaningless jargon or empty praise. Instead, use language that acknowledges individualism and creativity.

14. *Do you comment on children's appearance or clothing as "pretty" or "beautiful"?* What about the child who prefers comfort over style or does not have pretty clothes? Children need to know they are important and beautiful no matter how they look. Be sure to greet children at the door with an authentic good morning and without reference to their appearance. Show the children that who they are on the inside is what's most important.

15. *Do you call children by name?* Or do you overuse generic terms like "friend," "honey," and "sweetie"? Addressing children by name is one way to show respect and appreciation for them as individuals. Many adults have a habit of calling children by generic names and terms of endearment. Be aware that children may interpret these names differently than you do. In the book *Mommy Doesn't Know My Name* by Suzanne Williams, for example, a mother calls her daughter, Hannah, a variety of affectionate names. Hannah becomes convinced that her mommy does not know her name. Hannah envisions herself as a "pumpkin," a "chickadee," and so on, and keeps telling her mother, "I'm Hannah!"

This list offers just a sample of questions you can ask yourself while reflecting on your program. You can either ask these questions of yourself alone or share and ponder them with your colleagues.

PHOTO DOCUMENTATION

Photography is a valuable tool for observation, recording, and evaluation. With a digital camera and a memory card, you can take endless shots. You can edit and sort your photos later without the cost of film and developing. Digital cameras allow you to share photos and videos with children both immediately and later.

I once initiated a project exploring how to use digital photography in multiple ways as a valuable classroom tool. I wanted to find out what photography could mean to a busy classroom and its budding learners.

In the beginning, I photographed everything. This included everything the kids were doing, seeing, talking about, investigating, exploring, and so on. I photographed almost every art project, cooking project, science discovery, and experience in the natural world. I began to make amazing discoveries in the little events we'd been taking for granted. For example, I photographed and learned about the following:

- insects in the natural world and the children's faces while exploring the critters

- math and science, through measuring ice that we found and carrying it inside to continue measuring it as it melted

A large block of ice brought in for exploration

- more math and science, through lining up rocks and counting or making patterns with them

Counting rocks

- how children use materials, such as wet and dry clay

- discovery of materials, such as in ice cube painting

- how children use art materials and what they think and say, from first-time experiences to more advanced adventures

- the process and discoveries that happen in cooking projects

- sequences, through taking pictures as a process unfolds

Learning to see the process unfold

- children's individual development through the year

Note the child's grip and hand preference.

- how children use the environment and how they play

- what neighborhood happenings children see, such as construction being done on campus

Preparing to re-create a construction site

- daily routines, such as hand washing steps and snack steps

This list offers just a few examples of the many ways in which you can use photography in teaching two- and three-year-olds, as well as the many benefits photography provides. Chief among these benefits are the opportunities photography offers to truly reflect on your teaching and your students' learning and development.

CHAPTER 2

Strategies for Common Challenges

Many teachers of twos and threes struggle with the challenging situations and personalities that are common in this age group. Here are some behaviors typical of twos and threes that are or can be problematic:

- running
- climbing
- hitting
- pushing
- biting
- spitting
- grabbing items from other children
- hoarding toys
- resisting transitions
- short attention span
- trouble staying in circle
- trouble sitting at table for meals
- defiance
- anger
- tattling
- shyness
- lack of interest in peers, interest in adults only

Children and situations that challenge can be frustrating when you don't know how to deal with them or your efforts aren't working. This chapter aims to give you coping tools for handling the most common challenges, such as excess energy, aggression, building peer relationships, managing separations, easing transitions, and encouraging rest time.

Understanding your role as an educator in these situations is critical. It's your job to give children the social skills they need to become successful community members. The ability to help children solve problems, discover success, learn self-regulation, honor boundaries, use effective scripts, and develop respectful relationships with peers is an important teaching skill to develop. As you develop this skill, you build authentic and meaningful relationships with children.

Working with children and situations that challenge takes a lot of observation, reflection, and effort. Many of the challenges you face may appear similar to one another, but each challenge has a unique profile. It's important not only to learn a variety of coping strategies but also to know each child as an individual. When you really get to know a child, you can set better goals and create a plan that is suitable for that child. Understanding typical development is extremely important too. You need to have realistic expectations of the children's capabilities.

Here are a few general tips that apply to all challenging situations:

- Observe! Observe the child, the group dynamics, how the activities are unfolding, and how the environment affects behaviors.

- Identify the child's temperament, interests, and needs.

- Identify when the behaviors are occurring. Is there a pattern?

- Assess whether a problem behavior is typical for the child in question. If not, has something changed at home? For example, has the family moved, or have the parents separated? Is a family member ill? Has a pet died?

- Determine whether the child in question has a special need. Do you need input from a special education colleague?

- Reflect on how you have reacted to the challenge thus far.

- Ask yourself what you could do differently.

- Keep a journal and document your observations and actions. Note any patterns, the child or children who are involved, how often and when the behavior happens, and changes you implement, as well as their effect.

High Energy

I once had a student who was very energetic and who loved sports. He loved to kick, jump, and throw. He needed opportunities to move his whole body and to be successful. He also needed to channel his energy in ways that were creative, safe, healthy, and conducive to his temperament. It was tricky to balance his need for freedom with the need for safe boundaries. Among the strategies I developed was a kicking game. I made him a paper football

and taped a cardboard kicking tee and goal to the floor. We went through several footballs and tees that year. This game offered him a way to get the movement and achievement he needed in a safe, manageable way.

A paper football on a cardboard tee

A child moving his whole body

Through this experience and many others, I've learned that the key to success with active children is flexibility. Don't be too quick to say no or to impose a blanket rule. Instead, stop to think about a few things.

First, think about this particular child. What are his needs? How can you meet them?

Next, find out what the child's intentions are. Ask, "What is your plan?" or "What are you thinking about?" or "What will you be doing with those toys?"

Then ask yourself, "Is this safe? How can I make this a safe activity? What can I substitute that will help this child?"

Next, respond and reflect. Did your approach work? What else can you change?

Finally, set up a plan for this child. For example:

The child's interests are: *Construction.*

The child gets very active: *Right after circle time.*

Maybe I could try to: *Give him a quick moving activity before circle, then give him a Koosh ball to hold during circle, and have a building exercise waiting as soon as circle is over (blocks, hammer, tape).*

Other ideas are: *Offer him a tray with sand and vehicles, have an envelope with construction stickers and small papers available, make "personal space" activities available so other children do not get close for certain periods.*

Accomplishing a task

"Sawing" blocks

Hammering paper roof tiles

It's best to be proactive.

Here are some additional ideas for channeling excess energy. These work like magic!

- Play Nerf basketball.

- Use tape (regular or colored masking tape) to create roads, lines, and so on.

- Hammer golf tees into firm Styrofoam.

- Wash tables and chairs with small buckets of soapy water and sponges cut in half.

- Take a walk.

- Play with sand or water in individual or two-person bins.

Personal space is important.

- Tape plastic Easter eggs closed and bat them with empty paper towel rolls.

A simple, lightweight indoor activity

- Cut paper strips with safety scissors. (Keep a paper scrap box handy.)

- Offer a "big" job, such as lifting, carrying, or pushing. (For example: "Pedro, I have a job! I need some help! Can you help me move this pile?" Have Pedro help load blocks into a box,

basket, or wagon, and then push or pull it to another area.)

Big body work proves useful in many situations.

- Put colored masking tape on the underside of a table and ask the child to pull off the tape. If the child needs more time alone, invite her to put on more tape.

- Offer a variety of cardboard boxes for building, painting, taping, coloring, ripping, hammering golf tees, making houses, and so on.

Inside a box   *A dismantled box*

- Offer taped-together blocks for a child to "saw" apart.

- Offer a small, easily dismantled chair for a child to take apart and rebuild.

- Make available a long-running project for independent work, such as a roof on a classroom house.

Offering productive ideas is one great way to channel energy. Positive yet authentic messages are another powerful tool. Such messages help children feel respected and understood. And the more you use positive language, the more children will use it themselves. Children typically like to emulate and please adults. Here are some positive examples of language you can use as the energy rises:

- "It looks like you need a job!"

- "Are you needing to move your body?"

- "I wonder what would happen if…"

- "Hey! I have a great idea!"

- "I'm thinking about…"

Twos and threes may need to expend energy for various reasons. You may find children needing to release energy when they have not had enough opportunities for movement or when severe weather has prevented them from going outdoors. As teachers and caregivers, we need to find ways to help children get what their bodies need. Strategies that work for both particular children and the whole group are best.

. . . .

One snowy morning, a child decided to hurl a plastic baseball bat in the snow to watch it hit the snow and bounce into the air. Because he was a big presence within the group and other children often followed him, they tried to enter his space. He tried to tell the other children to stop following him, but they found his actions too compelling.

The teacher marked the child's space with bright sidewalk chalk in the trampled snow. This became his "safe zone," and others were not permitted to enter. The boundary protected others from the flying bat while giving the child the opportunity to explore, move, experiment, and feel powerful in his own personal space.

. . . .

Aggression

Aggression is a common issue for this age group. Twos and threes are still learning what appropriate behavior is, how to get along with others, and how to communicate in a social setting. Aggressive behaviors include hitting, biting, pushing, pulling hair, spitting, shouting, and grabbing. Observing and recording the behaviors will help you determine if a child's aggression falls within the typical range or if a bigger issue exists. Aggressive behaviors might indicate a concern you need to address. A child's home life may have taken an upsetting turn. Or perhaps something isn't working well for this child at school.

Sometimes aggression happens when the following situations occur:

- Not enough materials are available.

- The space is crowded.

- Children are bored or not challenged.

- Children cannot verbalize their frustrations or thoughts.

- Something happens to a child when you are not looking.

- Something else is going on in a child's life.

- A child has a special need that might require outside consultation.

After making careful observations, you can develop a plan to improve the situation. The environment is usually easier to fix, so start with environmental changes. If tweaking your schedule, methods, or environment does not improve aggression, try child-focused strategies next. Here are a few tips:

- Stay close by the child—or have someone else do so—to intervene if necessary.

- Help the child develop effective scripts and communication skills to get his needs met.

- Model and facilitate appropriate behaviors.

- Help the child feel supported, and assure that his needs are being met.

- Be certain other involved children can express their dislike for aggressive behaviors.

- Hold the aggressor accountable for inappropriate behaviors. Consistently send the message: "Aggression is not okay."

- If aggression continues, discuss it with the child's family to develop a consistent plan for home and school.

"I'M SORRY"

After an incident of aggression, I often hear teachers force children to say they are sorry to one another. Teachers often use apologies as rote statements to quickly end disputes. Adults may think that apologies are quick-and-easy problem solvers, but apologies actually have only a brief effect.

When taught to say, "I'm sorry," a young child will repeat the words and apologize. But how much meaning does this act really have for a two- or three-year-old? Does a child this young understand what the phrase means? Or does the child simply repeat it because she has been scolded and told to do so?

Apologizing seems like the polite and proper thing to have children do. But I don't believe in forcing children who aren't sorry to say that they are. I myself wouldn't say, "I'm sorry" if I really was not. The words would be meaningless and useless.

At age two or three, a child does not clearly understand the concept of remorse. A child needs to learn empathy before understanding how to be sorry. If children have not yet developed empathy, they learn nothing from apologizing except "If I say I am sorry, then all is well." For example: Sarah pushes Marcus down and Marcus cries. When Sarah sees a teacher coming to see if everyone is okay, she quickly shouts, "I said I was sorry!" Sarah has not learned anything about how Marcus was feeling, why it was wrong to push another child, or what to change in the future.

There are better ways to handle the aftermath of aggression. In this particular example, the teacher can approach the children and tend to any injuries first. The teacher can then question what happened and give both children a chance to explain. Next, the teacher could tell Sarah to look at Marcus's face and note how clearly upset he is. The teacher could say, "Let's ask Marcus if he is okay" or "Is there some way to help make Marcus feel better?" The teacher can validate Marcus's feelings and injuries, offering him a chance to say that it is not okay to push him. The teacher can then remind both children about the importance of safety, respecting personal space, and getting needs met in appropriate ways, such as asking for help, using words, and so on. Helping Marcus with this dialogue empowers him. His words have value and meaning. He knows the teacher is there to support him. And Sarah learns a meaningful and personal lesson.

Helping Children Build Relationships

As teachers, one of our most important jobs is to help children develop social skills and learn to get along well with others. We want to help children function as part of a group and a community.

Learning social skills is a key element of education for two- and three-year-olds. Little ones are naturally egocentric. It is hard work for them to learn that the world does not always revolve around them and that they cannot always have what they want when they want it.

Twos and threes must learn how to share space, materials, and experiences with other children. When you have a well-planned environment and curriculum, you open the door to successful social learning. This section will provide you with a variety of tools to help you achieve that goal.

SOCIAL BLOCKS

Social blocks are small, handheld blocks with photos of your students on them—one child per block. Small wooden unit blocks, such as the Mini Unit Blocks from Community Playthings, work well. These are the perfect size for small hands. Print photos of the children and cut them to the size of the blocks. Then affix the photos to the blocks with clear contact paper, transparent packing tape, or decoupage glue.

Two- and three-year-olds love to hold the blocks showing their own photos. For this reason, you might want to make two sets at a time: one set for the children to hold and the other set to leave at the social blocks play space. When a child really wants to have and hold the block with her photo on it, you should respect that desire. As the novelty of the social blocks wears off, so will the desire to carry them around.

You can use social blocks to aid your students in social interactions. The blocks are useful with both typical learners and children who have special needs. You may find social blocks especially helpful for children who, for reasons such as limited language development or shyness, lack peer interaction skills. Social blocks can help children acknowledge and communicate with one another.

Make the blocks at the beginning of the school year, as the children are learning names and getting to know one another. To begin using the blocks, demonstrate how to use them in conversational role play. Have the blocks interact and sustain conversations with one another. They can help you and the children model classroom scenarios.

For example, years ago when I had my family child care, I had a group heavy with four-year-olds. The fours were having a lot of peer conflicts, so we used the social blocks to aid in peer negotiations and developing empathy. When conflicts arose, I had children use their block people to say the words they wanted to say to other children (or to the other children's block people) until the children gained the skills they needed to negotiate effectively. This strategy worked quite well. Adaptions made to programs with younger children can result in successful benefits as well. The children absorbed a great deal of language and many social skills through these conversations.

Another way to use social blocks is for dramatizing stories and rhymes. For example, you might use the blocks with the nursery rhyme "There Was an Old Woman Who Lived in a Shoe." With a cardboard box, make a shoe-shaped house sculpture as an art project. Then use the shoe house and the social blocks to dramatize the nursery rhyme. When I tried this activity in my classroom, the result was amazing. One child who had rarely spoken at all began referring to the blocks by name and had them talk and play with one another. This activity led to a blossoming of her conversational skills that lasted the remainder of the school year. Another child who had little language or understanding of two-way language could use social blocks to initiate small intentional dialogues when sitting one-on-one with an adult who scaffolded language and peer recognition.

Social blocks

THE TIMID CHILD

Do you have a child in your group who seeks out only teachers for discussion and play? This is a very common issue among children without siblings and children who have high linguistic skills. Children without siblings may have little experience interacting with peers. And children with well-developed language skills may find it frustrating or confusing to interact with children who haven't yet developed those skills.

When you try to foster peer interactions, the child declines and turns back toward you. When peers attempt relationships with the child, their efforts fall short. As the peers mature and become more verbally adept, they give up on the child who keeps rebuffing them. This child, meanwhile, keeps pursuing adults. Adults are more predictable, responsive, and available for successful interaction than other children.

It is important to prevent such a child from dominating your time and attention. Every child needs individual time with you *and* with peers. When a child dominates your time, you are less available to other children. And when a child focuses solely on you, he misses out on important social experiences.

Keep this type of child in mind when you set up activities. For example, you could set up a train set or a block construction project big enough for several children. Next you might add a basket of figures, such as animals or people, that the child in question would like. You can begin the activity with that child and then encourage other children to join. Make sure the other children do not overpower the more timid child and take over the activity. Try to involve all the children cohesively. Encourage the children to pass things back and forth, exchanging both materials and language—even if you must initially speak for a child or help a child find the words necessary to get involved in the discussion. Build language and relationships by offering challenges that invite children to think and work together.

For instance, while building a train track, the children might lay straight pieces in a line. But curved pieces are necessary for making a loop the train can drive around. You say, "Uh-oh. Take a look ... the train will fall off the end of our track. How will we connect the ends?" The children look at it. One shouts, "We need to turn it!" You ask, "How will we turn it? What can we use?" A child says, "Use a curved piece." You hand a curved piece to the timid child and ask, "Could you please add

this to our track?" Then you hand the child another piece to pass to the next child.

The more you practice fostering relationships, the easier it will get. It will become a part of your mind-set. Here are some more suggestions for fostering early peer relationships:

- Pair up children with similar interests.

- Don't let more assertive children overpower more timid children.

- Give children the language they need to interact successfully with peers.

- Take interactions one at a time. Start with brief interactions, then build on each small positive experience.

- Think about peers who might make good playmates, and suggest a playdate to their families.

RESPECTFUL RELATIONSHIPS

As early childhood professionals, we know that relationships are the center of our work with young children and their families. But I think we need to reflect on how important those relationships truly are.

Forming authentic and respectful relationships with families is crucial to building trust. Families need to feel comfortable with your care and love for their children. They need to know that you have their children's best interest as your top priority. They need to believe you really understand their children, as well as their particular family's character, culture, and child-rearing style. Families need to know that you respect and value them. To achieve all this, you must take the time to make families feel welcome and listen carefully when they speak to you.

Children, too, need and deserve respect. Their youth and small size is no reason to treat them with anything less than full love, respect, and dignity. You can clearly tell when children know you understand them and are seeking to meet their individual needs. Respect toward children is about how we talk to them. Our words and demeanor show how we value them. They build a mutual relationship of respect and trust. Here are some tips for building respectful relationships with children:

- Get down on the children's level.

- Make direct eye contact with children.

- Use a soft touch to aid in bonding and to help children cope with emotions.

- Provide short, simple messages.

- Use nonjudgmental speech.

- Show kindness and warmth.

- Use a soft tone of voice.

- Use loving body language.

- Make unrushed time for conversation with children.

- Get to know the children and their families well.

- Be direct, have boundaries, and be consistent.

- Speak in positive instead of negative terms. For example, instead of saying, "Get down! No climbing on the furniture!" say, "Yikes! That doesn't look safe at all! Let's find a better climbing place!"

- Be adaptable and flexible.

- Remember that your job is to be not a playmate, but a guide and educator. Being too much of a playmate limits how the children play together. Establish your role carefully. Set the stage for role play, facilitate peer relationships, and guide with toys and materials—and then step back and encourage children to take over.

SOCIAL SCRIPTS

Social scripts can help you develop respectful language and tone within your classroom and build a foundation for effective peer negotiations and successful relationships. Modeled scripts establish a consistent flow of conversation and set conversational and behavioral expectations.

Following are many scripts and sentence starters you can use often within the classroom. Try these, if they're applicable, or create your own using these scripts as a model. In all communications with children, make your face and tone match your message. And whenever you give a message, follow through on it.

- "I see that you are feeling angry. I know that waiting for a turn can be hard."

- "If you are thinking about a turn, let Donovan know. When he is all done, he will give you a turn. What should we do while we are waiting?"

- "I see that you are upset, and my message is…"

- "I see that you are upset. Is there a message you want to tell me?"

- "I have a message for you."

- "Take a look at Natasha. It sounds like she has a message for you."

- "Take a look at her face. She doesn't look happy."

- "I'm thinking about…"

- "I know you are thinking about (or playing with) _____, but it's just not a choice right now."

- "It looks as though you are feeling angry. Let's try to work this out."

- "I see you are feeling angry. I would like to help you."

- "It makes me worry when…"

- "I'm going to have to say that is not a safe choice."

- "So I am wondering… what you are thinking about?"

- "Use your words to give him your message."

- "When you throw your food, you are telling me you are all done eating."

- "When you are not sitting, it tells me you are ready to leave (be done)."

- "So I am noticing that…"

- "I am reminding you that when we are in the hall, we need a teacher's hand."

- "So I am reminding you that when we walk in the parking lot, we *always* need an adult's hand. We need to keep our bodies safe."

- "This just doesn't look safe to me."

- "Stop your body—that does not look safe."

- "Are you thinking you might like a turn? Let's let Kenzie know."

- "If you walk away, that says the toy is available."

- "If no one's hands are on the toy, that says it is available."

- "You can let Kathy know you are using it, and when you are all done, it will be her turn."

- "It sounds like you are shouting. You can use your talking voice."

- "You are shouting at me. Let me know in a softer voice what you are thinking."

- "Let Seun know… give him your message."

- "Hold on. I need you to stop your body. Giovanni has a message for you."

- "Take a look at my face! My face does *not* look happy."

- "I have a *serious* message for you."

- "I need you to hear my words."

- "That is *not* okay. You need to…"

- "So I am letting you know that in two minutes, it will be your turn for a diaper change. In two minutes I will be back for your turn."

- "In two minutes, it will be time to clean up to go outside."

- "Let's find out if that is okay with Simone. Simone, is it okay if Michael knocks down your blocks? Do you like it when he does that? No? Then you can tell him to stop."

- "You can tell him, 'Stop. I don't like that.'"

- "You can tell her, 'It's my turn.'"

- "You can tell him, 'I need some space. You're too close.'"

- "So here is the thing…"

- "Right now, your job is to…"

- "This is your job. You need to…"

- "It's not a choice. You need to wash your hands to eat."

- "Your choice is a diaper change before or after snack. Which do you prefer?"

- "I like the way you asked—thank you!"

- "I like the way you passed the napkins."

- "I like the way you said that. What nice manners!"

- "I like the way you shared. How friendly!"

- "I like the way you…"

- "How kind of you!"

- "You are a good friend!"

- "This shows you are really growing up! Wow!"

- "I noticed you are really waiting patiently. Good for you!"

- "Do you just need a minute to yourself?"

- "You could just say, 'No, thank you.'"

- "I'm letting you know I don't like that. It hurts me when you hit my leg."

- "This looks like a problem. Let's see how we can work things out."

- "This is a real problem. We need to talk about this."

- "You are not listening to my words."

- "You can do it yourself, or I can help you."

- "So if you are not doing it, it will be my choice to help you do it."

- "This is a really tricky problem. This makes me worry."

- "It looks like you are having trouble. I'd like to help you."

In these scripts, notice the key phrases *I'm noticing, I'm wondering, I am thinking, I have a message for you, it looks as though, it sounds like, this looks like a problem,* and so on. These phrases are helpful because they form a consistent base of communication. They open up the conversation with a respectful tone, help children articulate their needs and negotiate with peers, and get right to the issue at hand. The scripts establish clear boundaries about what is acceptable and what is not. Some are quick attention grabbers for important messages that follow.

"FRIENDS"

Teachers and other adults often refer to young children in a group as "friends." For example, a teacher might say, "Give your friend Harry a turn!" or "We are all friends in this classroom," or "Come on, friends, it's time to line up!" or "Friends, I need you to listen." We might just slip into this habit, or we might pick it up from others. I've thought about it a lot over the years, and it still perplexes me.

Children aren't automatically friends simply because they are the same age and belong to the same group. They are peers and classmates. They need to be *friendly* toward one another, but they need not consider one another as friends unless the feeling is authentic. We all—adults and children—like certain people and feel less warm about other people. Are we doing children a disservice by confusing the concept of classmate with the concept of friend? We should respect children as individuals with valid preferences and emotions. If a child does not wish to be called someone's friend or does not choose to have that person as a friend, then we should honor that choice.

By the same token, I question whether we as professionals should be calling children our friends. Are they our friends? Are we their playmates? What might some alternatives be? Perhaps it would be better to use the more correct terms *children* or *everyone.*

Separations

Morning separations can be difficult for young children. Some children have more frequent trouble with separations than other children do. In addition, personal circumstances might affect a child's entrance into the classroom. For example, reentry can be hard after a long weekend, when a child is tired or not feeling well, when a family member is away from home for business, or when changes are occurring at home.

To ease separations, it's extremely important to know the child well and work closely with the family. Use your knowledge and your good relationship to set up a quick, personal activity to help a child feel comfortable or express herself. For example, you might try the following. (In addition, see the separation tips on page 12.)

- Offer your lap and a picture book for one-on-one story time.

- Guide the child to the writing table and offer to write down his feelings.

- Direct the child to a bin with soapy water, ducks, and scoops.

- Give the child playdough plus a hammer and golf tees.

Playing with soapy water, ducks, and scoops is a soothing activity for younger children.

Supply markers and leftover gak on a tray. To explain his feelings when she left that morning, a child wanted a message written on a note, as shown in this photo.

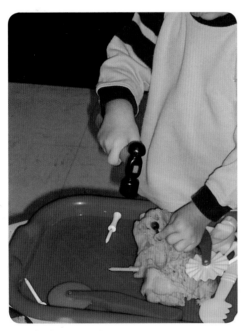

Playdough and a hammer and golf tees offer an excellent alternative use.

Transitions

Transitions can be stressful for anyone, including a child. And in a classroom of twos and threes, transitions can quickly turn chaotic with high energy and mayhem!

To manage transitions successfully, we need to have reasonable expectations for this age group. Transitions cannot be too complex. Wait times between activities should be within children's capabilities and should not be spent standing in line. Consistent and familiar transition routines help children know what to expect and what you expect from them.

When a transition begins to fall apart, you need to think and act fast. Silliness and other unwanted behaviors are contagious! Always be prepared for an unexpected wait or a change in plans. Here are some ideas you can use to gain children's attention and pass time productively:

- Give ample and repeated warnings before a transition. For example: "In five minutes . . . ," "In two minutes . . . ," and "It's just about time . . ."

- Use enticing language that will make children stop and listen to you. For example, say, "I have something really exciting to tell [show] you…" or "You *won't* believe this!"

- Split the group. Take whoever is ready onward rather than making them wait.

- Recite familiar chants or rhymes while waiting.

- Play simple games to keep the children's attention.

- Play a "follow me" game while waiting. Say, "If you are ready, put your hands on your head! Put them on your tummy! Put your finger on your nose!" and so on.

- Whisper to get the children's attention. They will want to hear your "secret," so they will often quiet down to hear you.

- Tell the children, "Put your goggles on!" Put on pretend goggles, look around, and talk about what you see.

- Play a game of I Spy. You begin by giving the children a clue so they can guess what visible object you're thinking of: "I spy with my little eye… something blue!" After someone guesses correctly, let the children take turns as the spy.

- Give the children a mission to hunt for something. For example, say, "Workers! We have a job! We need to search for…!"

- Tell stories or read a book while waiting.

- Listen to an audio book.

- Do a quick music-and-movement activity.

- Give children plenty of visuals and visual cues.

- Make lists with the names of children who are waiting for a turn. Children can see their names, know their turns are coming, develop patience, and learn about taking turns and fairness. Be certain that each waiting child is offered a turn, even if he has found a new activity in the meantime.

- Sing songs while you're waiting. (See the following examples.)

TRANSITION SONGS

Transition songs are a quick way to help young children to focus and wait. They are a positive and developmentally appropriate activity before moving on to the next activity or routine step in their day. Transition songs aid in a smooth transition for young children.

Found a Pumpkin

(Tune: "Found a Peanut")
Found a pumpkin, found a pumpkin,
Found a pumpkin on the ground.
Michael came along and picked it, took it
    home and said, "It's mine!"
(Continue with all the children's names.)

Ten in the Bed

There were ten in the bed, and the little one
    said, "Roll over! Roll over!"
So they all rolled over, and one fell out.
There were nine in the bed…
(Continue counting down to one.)
There was one in the bed, and the little one
    said,
(Tune: "He's Got the Whole World in His Hands")
"I've got the whole bed to myself, I've got the
    whole bed to myself,
I've got the whole bed to myself! I've got the
    whole bed to myself!"

Two Little Blackbirds

Two little blackbirds sitting on a hill. *(Begin
    with both hands behind your back.)*
One named Jack. *(Bring the first hand out with
    pointer finger extended.)*
One named Jill. *(Bring the second hand out
    with pointer finger extended.)*
Fly away Jack. *(Put the first hand behind your
    back.)*
Fly away Jill. *(Put the second hand behind your
    back.)*
Come back Jack. *(Bring first hand back.)* Come
    back Jill! *(Bring second hand back.)*

Little Cabin in the Woods

In a cabin by the wood, *(Make a cabin shape with pointer fingers.)*

By the window a little man stood. *(Hold hand over eyebrow looking out.)*

He saw a rabbit hopping by, *(Hold up two fingers like rabbit ears; hop hand up and down.)*

Knocking at the door. *(Make a fist and motion knocking at the door.)*

"Help me, help me," the rabbit cried. *(Open and shut hands twice.)*

"I just need a place to hide." *(Slide hands in front of face to hide.)*

"Come little rabbit, come inside. *(Make "come" hand motion.)*

I'll take care of you!" *(Cross arms to simulate rocking a baby.)*

Twinkle, Twinkle, Little Star

Twinkle, twinkle, little star.
How I wonder what you are.
Up above the world so high,
Like a diamond in the sky!
Twinkle, twinkle, little star.
How I wonder what you are.

Movement Song

Sally, Sally, jump up and down, jump up and down, jump up and down.

Sally, Sally, jump up and down, then—sit—back—down!

If You're Ready and You Know It

(Tune: "If You're Happy and You Know It")
If you're ready and you know it, clap your hands!
If you're ready and you know it, clap your hands!
If you're ready and you know it, and you really want to show it,
If you're ready and you know it, clap your hands!

Rest Time and Quiet Time Strategies

Some children love rest and *need* rest. They are quick to fall asleep peacefully. Some children want to sleep and are visibly tired but cannot relax enough to rest. Other children fight sleep. It is apparent they are tired, but each time they begin to relax, they jar their bodies and wake themselves.

Resting peacefully

Remember that the classroom environment is nothing like the bedroom a child sleeps in at home. Certain children have difficulty adapting to this difference. To help all your children rest, it is important that you create a peaceful atmosphere conducive to resting. It is equally important that you get to know each child's resting habits and preferences. This knowledge can help you create a rest plan that works for each individual.

Here are some ideas for creating a peaceful rest room:

- Darken the room—but not too dark for licensing regulations.

- Play soft, peaceful music (without lyrics) or nature sounds.

- Switch on some white noise such as from a fan or air purifier.

- Keep the room at a comfortable temperature.

- Provide comfortable mats and bedding. Make sure you have spare bedding for borrowing if parents forget or if you need extra covers.

- Prior to resting, have a reading time to help relax the children. Provide rest-time book baskets.

- Offer back rubs (or forehead stroking, hair stroking, or other preference of child), rocking, or holding to help children get relaxed.

- Sing or hum if that's helpful to a particular child.

- Lie down alongside the children as they get comfortable for their resting period. Snuggles are often welcome!

- Find out from families how children rest at home (for naps and bedtime).

- Place mats strategically, according to types of sleepers and needs of individual children. Keep tweaking your mat layout until you find one that works well.

- Reduce stimuli for children who need it. For example, put a child in a quieter area or in a corner, or block views from a room with a spare mat or two chairs with a sheet draped across them.

- Have a "rest buddy" basket with clean spare stuffed animals to offer the children. Be sure to wash the animals afterward. If children have favorites they like to use repeatedly, just leave favorites in their cubbies when packing up after rest early in the week, and then wash the animals at the end of the week and put them back in the basket of spares.

- Encourage children to bring snuggly comfort items from home, such as blankets, stuffed animals, and baby dolls.

- Keep music and white noise steady throughout the rest time so sound is consistent. Keep other noises and disturbances muffled.

- As children wake, or as rest time ends, lighten the room gradually and lower the music gently. Provide a thoughtful and comforting wake-up period. No one wants to wake to loud noises and bright lights. Make sure the adults in the room, as well as the children, show courtesy toward those who are still resting or waking.

- Mark on cubby baskets what goes home each day. (For example: "Send home Johnny's bear and blanket each night.")

- If a child uses a pacifier, ask the family to provide a spare pacifier. Store it in a ziplock bag for emergencies.

QUIET BAGS

Not all two- and three-year-olds take naps. At this age, some children may begin to drop their naps during the school year. We need to be respectful of nonnapping children's needs. Although we must follow state-mandated "rest period" rules, after that mandated period, we can provide an activity for nonsleepers.

Quiet bags offer children who do not sleep something quiet to do while other children are sleeping. They provide these children with an opportunity to relax and rest while remaining quiet as a courtesy to the children who need to sleep. Quiet bags also honor the fact that a rest period is a valuable time for the teacher to get things done. A soothing rest room is important for all the children and adults, and quiet bags help make that environment possible.

Quiet bags are an incentive. Children can look forward to playing with quiet bags during rest time. The rule is that one must be quiet in order to have one. When you use quiet bags, you are teaching an important skill. You are helping children learn to regulate and rest themselves, which is healthy for their minds and bodies.

Here are some ideas for things to include in a quiet bag:

- paper booklets stapled together

- notepads

- colored pencils (not markers, which will get on bedding)

- stickers

- small puzzles

- lacing cards

- Beanie Babies

- finger puppets

- miniature Etch A Sketch

- small books or book basket

- felt sets

- small Magna Doodle

All items in quiet bags should be things a child can use independently, quietly, and safely. Rotate the items in quiet bags each week to hold the children's interest. Remind children that a quiet bag is a treat, and they need to lie quietly and rest a bit first. A restful period of even thirty minutes is healthy for any child in child care. Store quiet bags in a shoe box, a plastic bin, or a large binder.

A quiet basket

A quiet bag

CHAPTER 3

Creative and Authentic Art

Art for younger children should focus on the process, not the product. *Process over product* is a phrase you've probably heard often as a teacher. Take a few minutes to really think about what it means: that we should encourage children to explore art materials and enjoy the process of exploration. For a two- or three-year-old, exploration means asking and answering questions about art materials, such as "Can I touch it? What does it feel like? What happens if I use more?" It is more important for children to have meaningful, exciting, and developmentally appropriate art experiences than it is to produce a product at the end.

For this age group, art is a very sensory experience. Young children seek input from art materials, and getting input often involves using their hands. Twos and threes really enjoy touching, feeling, and squeezing art materials. They may also be curious about the taste of art materials. It is typical for twos and young threes to put items in their mouths. That's why safety and adult supervision are very important. Careful observation and knowledge about each individual child will help you determine what materials are safe for your group of children to explore.

Young children need many opportunities for experimentation with different kinds of art and different kinds of media. Art projects should be open-ended, with as little teacher direction as possible. Accept that art exploration will be quite messy. Remember that hands-on exploration is the most meaningful and productive way for children to learn. Embrace the adventure and excitement, the fun and the challenge!

Reflecting on Your Role

As you plan art experiences for young children, you must understand not only the children in your group, but also yourself. You need to learn about different art media, styles, approaches, and processes. You need to try new things and step back and observe what happens. Then you need to examine your comfort level. You need to be comfortable with what you offer and decide what—if any—boundaries you will place on the children's art experiences.

It takes time and patience to let children freely experience and create art at their own pace and under their own direction. Sometimes the sensory experience is all a child may be interested in—not a finished product. Such situations may challenge your personal comfort or your beliefs about art education. Just as we teachers offer children new learning experiences, we ourselves face new challenges, learning opportunities, and experiences alongside the children.

Art exploration is a great way to understand your own ideas and limitations. Try to be open-minded, reflective, and thoughtful about your teaching practice as you experience art with your students. Different teachers have widely varying comfort zones. Sharing your thoughts with coteachers may be helpful in defining or broadening your art boundaries.

Child-Directed versus Cookie-Cutter Art

Independent decision making and free use of art materials can be difficult for adults to adapt to. But they are vitally important for young learners!

Early on, try to impress upon your children that they are in charge of their art explorations. Ask them, "What will you do?" Remind them, "You are the artist!"

Although you may set out the materials, and you may have a general idea of what children will do with them, ultimately you should leave it up to the children. They may try out the project as presented, or they may come up with their own ideas. Children often choose the latter when they have the freedom to do so. It doesn't take long for children to understand that they really are artists and that their creativity lies within their own hands.

The central question I always ask children is "What is your plan?" If they can answer that question, then I say, "Go for it!" Some children don't understand that question right away. So I ask, "Well, what will you do with that paint? What is the plan?" Then they get it! Soon they develop a goal and de-

cide how to get to it. The goal may be simply to explore, and the plan may change several times. I ask them about their plan just to get them thinking consciously about what they are doing. I stretch my questions as far as I can to help children develop creativity and confidence.

If you let them, children will come up with goals and develop plans to achieve them. (They will master execution of an idea.) Enjoy the process of children's art. Enjoy the way they experiment, question, plan, and develop understanding. Without jumping in to answer, listen to their questions and musings: "Hmm, what color paint do I want?" "What color will it make if I mix these together?" "Let's mix this and this and see what happens!"

Cookie-cutter art is the opposite of child-directed art. It involves shapes that teachers design and provide for children to decorate. But decoration is all this is. It is neither art nor education.

A classroom festooned with twelve cute, nearly identical teddy bears is a reflection of the teacher, not the children. The same is true of coloring sheets, coloring books, and all adult-designed materials indicating exactly what children should do. A child cannot exercise creativity or learn anything meaningful from such projects. In fact, cookie-cutter art leads young children to believe that all art should look the same and that it should look how the teacher wants it to look. It limits children's learning and stifles their creativity. Cookie-cutter art is not developmentally appropriate for preschoolers or younger children.

Art should give children the opportunity to be creative and to produce original work. It should employ authentic materials and inspire trial and error. True art develops confidence, a love of art, and critical-thinking and problem-solving skills. As teachers and caregivers, we have a responsibility to foster these important skills every time we invite children to the art area.

· ·

One student of mine rarely came to the art center at the beginning of the year. I suspected that his interest simply lay in other areas. Art wasn't exciting enough. He was a very busy boy! He loved moving his body around. Art seemed too quiet and confining to him.

That changed when I offered him the power to choose his materials and what to do with them. From that day forward, he often came to the art center independently. He came because my squirt bottles of paint intrigued him. He had never experienced such freedom with paint and artistic endeavors. He squirted and blobbed paint with curiosity and excitement! He kept waiting for me to say, "Okay, stop!" When I didn't, he was even more exhilarated. As the year progressed, he became interested in mixing colors and continued to explore how much he could possibly do with the materials.

. . . .

Making Art Inviting

How do we keep children coming to the art center? How do we keep the art center fresh, exciting, and full of age-appropriate art activities that build a love for creativity and artistic exploration?

First we must observe children carefully to see what their abilities and interests are. A thoughtful teacher or caregiver can address these factors, providing repetition to increase confidence and skill while introducing new materials and techniques.

Following are some tips to make your art center inviting:

- Use children's favorite colors or colors that attract them.

- Add materials that you know children enjoy, such as trucks.

- Arrange materials in an aesthetically pleasing and inviting way.

- Be attentive, enthusiastic, and interested in the children's art. Make everything sound exciting!

- Be flexible and willing to adapt to the children's needs and desires.

- Be aware of the developmental stages children are going through.

- Appreciate every moment—including the umpteenth time children want to paint with their hands!

- Try not to worry about the mess.

- Let the children make decisions and let them be the ones completing each step of the process.

- Be creative and foster creativity in the children. Offer choices and allow full exploration of materials.

Watching the paint drip down

Outdoor fingerpainting—with sand from the sandbox unexpectedly mixed in

Splatter painting!

Covering the whole sheet of paper—and hands too!

How can we present art materials to young children in an age-appropriate and explorative manner? It can be difficult to find the balance between letting children experiment and worrying about creating a giant mess or wasting materials. It is true that the early stages of art exploration are often messy and indulgent. But what the children learn through mess and indulgence is priceless.

Whether your art center is in its infancy or is the product of years of experience, you can always learn more about early art education. I recommend exploring other ways to invite children to explore and create beyond what you currently do. You can get new ideas through books, colleagues, workshops, or the Internet.

Art can be a simple planned activity that goes according to our finest expectation. Examples of fun experiences include two types of ice cube painting, one with liquid watercolor and the second with thicker tempera paint. This activity can lead to wonderful discoveries and differences detected in the consistency of melting paint cubes.

Art can be unexpected too. "Ooh, I did not think of that—but wow, look what he is doing!" As a child painted on a canvas with rubber brayers, the brayers reminded him of one of our previous art activities, monoprinting. He then began scraping designs and making prints. I thought it was great he had recalled the project and turned this project into his own idea. So I went with it!

And then there are those art moments that make many grown-ups cringe!

. . . .

This project evolved in a completely unintended way. And that was half the fun!

I had planned to have the children wear backward smocks with lamb's tails attached to represent the lamb in their daily nursery rhyme, "Little Bo Peep." But wearing the smocks did not appeal to the children in this particular group.

So we ripped off the tails and used them as paintbrushes. Most of the children dipped the tails in their choice of paint and gently painted with them. But one child had his own ideas. He said, "I have a plan! I need to put the paper on the floor like this." Then he began dipping his lamb's tail in paint, lifting it up, and whipping it to the ground! The tail left colorful splatters of vibrant colors on the large sheet of paper. It also decorated the walls, the furniture, and the hair and clothing of those nearby.

When he looked a bit nervous about the splattering, I simply moved the other children out of the way and asked the splattering child, "Well, who is the artist?" He replied with a smile, *"Me!"*

Painting with a lamb tail

. . . .

Collaborative Art

Children can learn many things through collaborating on art projects. They get a chance to exercise their large muscles when they produce big artworks together. They build community in the classroom. They learn how to work together in a confined area, sharing space and materials. They get many opportunities to practice problem solving.

If two children want to use the same paintbrush or the same paint color, they can learn strategies for sharing materials. The teacher could scaffold this learning by steering the conversation. For example: "Linnea, when you are all done with the pink paint, will you pass it to Maddie, please? She would like a turn when you are finished. Maddie, would you like to use purple while you are waiting?"

If a child paints on top of another child's work,

the children can learn strategies for sharing space. The teacher could remind the children that this is a group project, and all the classmates are working together. Perhaps the child who wants more space could move to a less crowded space near a teacher. If working together is too difficult that day for the child who wants more space, the teacher could offer the child a small sheet of paper for solo painting.

Through collaborative art, children develop understanding of space and proximity. They develop a plan together and work together to carry out the plan. The artwork hangs on the wall for all to see and take pride in.

To Smock or Not to Smock

Is this a crazy question to ask? Even if it seems ridiculous, it's still a worthwhile question if it helps us reflect on our teaching practice.

Many teachers require children to wear smocks if they wish to engage in art. And indeed, insisting that children wear smocks for messy work seems practical and logical. So what's the problem? Younger children and children with sensory issues often do not want to wear smocks. Many children will avoid art altogether if the smock is nonnegotiable.

If you notice this happening in your classroom, you might want to offer the children a choice about wearing smocks. Be aware, though, that optional smocking makes some adults uncomfortable. Explain your philosophy clearly to families as soon as possible. It's better to let a child get messy and have an artistic experience than to let a child miss out on the experience because he won't wear a smock. Remind families to dress their children in clothing that can get messy.

You may still want to encourage the children to wear smocks or aim toward the goal of wearing smocks if mess is likely. You can also make the children aware of their clothing as they begin to get messy. You may choose to change them—or simply let them go home "colorful." But one thing is certain: the children will enjoy their artistic endeavors! Don't be surprised to see an increase in art center attendance if you relax your smock-wearing rules.

Tip! **Keep wet sponges, baby wipes, or paper towels at the ready for quickly cleaning the children's hands or work areas. Having a soapy bucket of water on hand is also quite useful while messy projects are happening!**

Painting

When you invite young children to paint, offer a variety of implements, paints, paint additives, and painting surfaces. A wide variety of painting materials exist, and each has a different feel and produces a different effect. Don't forget that everyday items can double as painting materials, offering new and fun ways to paint! Use trial and error to find out what works well for your children and what does not.

IMPLEMENTS

What can we paint with?

- paintbrushes in different sizes, textures, and thicknesses
- foam brushes
- sponges in various sizes and shapes
- cotton swabs
- cotton balls
- foam rollers
- brayers or rubber rollers
- rollers for edges or trim (from a hardware store)
- spools
- fingers
- eyedroppers
- toothbrushes
- containers with shaker tops for powdered paint
- spray bottles

- ice cubes frozen in ice cube trays
- ice pops frozen in molds
- pine needles
- squirt bottles
- balloons
- carpet squares
- paint scrapers, flat and designed or textured (from an art supply store)
- toy cars and trucks
- toy trains and train tracks
- plastic toy animal feet
- Koosh balls
- keys
- large marbles
- golf balls
- turkey basters
- flyswatters
- potato mashers
- spatulas
- berry baskets (from produce department)
- feather dusters
- tea bags
- corks
- containers and lids
- kitchen scrubbers
- shoes or boots
- mittens
- string or yarn
- hands and feet

Tip! **When painting with cotton balls, use clothespins to hold the cotton balls if children are sensitive to messy paint on their hands. Clothespins work well for small sponges too.**

Tip! **Assemble a recycled items donation wish list to give to families. Items may include sturdy containers, lids, small trays, empty paper towel tubes, small boxes, large boxes, flat cardboard, craft materials, fabric, towels, sheets, or tablecloths. Choose donations carefully. Taking too much will just build clutter.**

Storage

You can store painting implements in a variety of ways, such as on shelves or in boxes, bins, or silverware sorters. If your classroom is cluttered and crowded, you may need a storage space that's out of the way. Try a clear plastic shoe holder that hangs from the top of a door. You can find this type of shoe organizer at a department store or home improvement store. Each shoe pocket can hold a different type of painting implement. The implements are not only neatly organized but also easily visible through the plastic. And best of all, young children can't dump this kind of storage container!

A hanging shoe holder used for brushes and rollers

PAINTING CONTAINERS

If you're using different kinds of painting implements, you'll also need different kinds of containers to hold paint and water. When the children are painting with brushes, good containers might be baby food jars, baby food plastic containers and lids, yogurt cups and lids, and inexpensive plastic storage containers. When the children are painting with rollers or brayers, good paint containers might be plastic trays from microwave or takeout food.

To make containers for when the children are painting with cotton swabs, cut clear egg cartons into sections of four compartments each. Put a different color of paint into each compartment. You might also use a divided plate to hold paint.

TYPES OF PAINT

Explore art with a variety of paints! Try tempera paint, puffy paint (foam paint), fingerpaint, watercolor cakes, liquid watercolors, corn syrup paint (created by adding a small amount of corn syrup to food coloring), powder paint (be cautious about allergies), and more. (See appendix B for several paint recipes.)

Tempera paints work especially well for two- and three-year-olds. Early on, just offer two or three colors, preferably the primary colors red, yellow, and blue. The children may choose to use primary colors alone or mix them to create secondary colors. A bit later, add white for tinting. Next, add black for shading. This strategy offers children the opportunity to explore art with an array of colors, shades, and tints.

Mixing colors is a great learning experience for young children. Through experimentation, they increase their understanding of colors. As time passes and children have more experiences with paint and with blending colors, they become more comfortable and confident.

To facilitate learning, help children keep the base colors separate by providing small containers or paper plates for mixing. It is too difficult for young children to mix paint right on their paper. And many children will not be interested in painting if you mix the colors for them. Mixing is half the fun for most children!

Paint Additives

Adding other ingredients to paint can have dramatic results. Here are some additive ideas: salt, glitter, sand, dirt, mud, vegetable oil, baby oil, water, dishwashing detergent, condensed milk, sawdust, and coffee grounds.

PAINTING SURFACES

Children can paint on a variety of surfaces. Here are just a few: large butcher paper, canvas, watercolor paper, drawing paper, fingerpainting paper, aluminum foil, waxed paper, poster board, newspapers, brown paper grocery bags, computer paper, cardboard, boxes, empty paper towel tubes, sculptures, and so on.

Tip! **Wrap aluminum foil, white tissue paper, or waxed paper around pieces of poster board. The poster board makes a sturdy painting surface for delicate materials.**

The Easel

The classroom easel is a crucial part of a twos-and-threes classroom. It should be available every day for use in a variety of ways with a variety of materials. Here are some items to keep handy at your easel:

- two or three paint cups with one brush in each

- watercolor or tempera cakes

- water in a small container next to the paint cakes (or a small squirt bottle for moistening the paint cakes)

- writing implements, such as crayons, markers, pencils, and oil pastels

- chalk, dry or wet

- liquid watercolors (in heavy glass baby food jars to prevent spills)

- bingo stampers or other liquid stampers

- paper, foil, and canvas of assorted sizes and types

- a variety of painting implements

And here are some tips for a successful easel:

- Arrange the easel in an attractive manner.

- Limit easel work to one or two children per side.

- Have a camera, pencil, and notepad readily available.

- Have towels or cleanup material handy, particularly for the floor.

A freshly covered easel

Foil-covered papers and glitter paint

Painting at the classroom easel

Painting at the table as a group

Using individual easels at the table

Using individual trays at the table

Tip To ease cleanup and to preserve your easel, wrap the easel in newspaper covered with waxed paper. Secure the paper with masking tape. The waxed paper speeds cleanup and shortens the time needed to change newspaper. If you like, wrap the easel tray in foil for easy cleanup.

MARBLE PAINTING

Marble painting creates amazing artwork. It's a favorite among twos and threes, and you can adapt this project in various ways.

First, you will need containers to hold paint and marbles. The containers should be wide enough for a child to scoop out marbles easily. A plastic spoon works well for scooping. Provide one spoon per paint container. Do not use typical glass marbles with younger children; they are too small and present a choking hazard. Instead, use very large marbles, golf balls, cat toy balls, small Wiffle balls, or rubber bouncy balls.

Next, choose a tray to hold the paper. The tray can be any shallow container with sides, such as a cafeteria tray, a box lid, a food storage container, or a cake pan. For a group marble-painting project, use a large box or a textured table insert.

Have the child put a marble or ball in the paint of choice, then scoop out the ball and drop it into the tray. Then have the child tip the tray to make the ball roll back and forth, creating colored lines across the paper. The child can decide how much paint to use, how many balls to use, and how long to shake, tilt, and roll the tray.

Golf ball painting in a box lid

In a pizza box!

In an oatmeal can using a cat toy ball

Tip! Use a closed box or container to prevent marbles from flying around the room, for a change of pace, or when you want children to shake the boxes and hear the marbles inside. Oatmeal containers, pizza boxes, and food storage containers can be closed easily. Tape paper to the inside of the box.

CANVAS PAINTING

Painting on canvas is often a new and wonderful experience for young children. It gives them a foundation for using authentic art materials.

Use small canvases for individual work or a large framed canvas for group projects. Either way, you can paint several different layers on the same canvas over several days.

If you use typical school tempera paint, you can wash the paint off the canvas with warm running water and a small brush. You can then bring out new paint for the children and begin again! Another way to start anew is to paint black paint over an old painting or freshly washed canvas to create a blank space for a new painting. (Let the black paint dry before painting.) Acrylic black paint will resist blending with new colors painted over it.

Canvas painting

TAPE RESIST

Tape resist is a fun project that you can adapt to make a new activity every time. Have children arrange tape on canvas or poster board to make lines and designs. (The best kinds of tape to use are colored tape from a school supply store or carpenter tape from a hardware store.) Then give the children rollers, brayers, or brushes to paint over the whole surface with a variety of colors. When the paint is dry, carefully lift off the tape to reveal the white lines and designs within the painting. The first time you do this project, the children will be amazed!

Tape resist

CRAYON RESIST

Crayon resist is similar to tape resist. Use white crayons for a surprise effect, or use oil pastels for a more obvious effect. Give children the crayons or oil pastels and let them color their pictures. When they're finished coloring, have them use small or medium-size paintbrushes to paint liquid paint over the drawing. The waxy or oily drawing will repel the paint, creating a striking artwork.

SPLATTER PAINT

Splatter painting is an exciting classroom project. This style of painting is carefree, fun, and creative. It does, however, become very messy! It involves dipping long paintbrushes into the paint and whipping the paint freely toward the painting surface. You can do splatter painting using a few different techniques.

Splatter painting

Paper within a box works especially well. Use a medium-size or large box with sides up to twenty-four inches tall (no higher than children's underarms). The sides keep the paint inside the box and help prevent a huge mess. Line the bottom of the box with paper and tape it down. Invite the children to come over one or two at a time to paint.

You will need at least three colors of paint, slightly watered down, and three to five long-handled, slim paintbrushes. The paint containers should be heavy so they won't tip over. The children can dip the brushes in the paint and fling the paint into the box. They can fling free style or tap the handle of the paintbrush on the side of the box or on the backs of their hands. This is a standing art activity. And it's really fun to photograph!

Following are a few additional tips for splatter painting:

- Canvas works well for splatter painting, too, and it creates a lasting piece of art. Canvas can be costly, though, which limits the use of this option in most classrooms.

- Poster board is a great alternative to canvas. It is not as expensive, but it is very durable. Also, with poster board, you can turn it over after it dries and use the reverse side for new work.

- You can do splatter painting as a second-day effect. On the first day of the project, for example, have the children paint with rollers. On the second day, after the base paint is dry, add the splatter painting.

- For very big splatter paintings, use large butcher paper. Try this outdoors, hanging the paper on a fence or laying it on the ground.

- Large twelve-by-eighteen-inch paper taped together works well too.

Splatter painting in a big box

Tip! After painting on canvas, I decided to reuse the canvas for another painting. I felt a bit sad to cover the children's artwork, but I knew it was worth it to have another painting experience. During a nursery rhyme unit, we painted the canvas all black to make a night sky background. Then we splatter-painted the canvas to represent the song "Twinkle, Twinkle, Little Star." The results were stunning!

Splatter painting on a black canvas

Splatter painting with both hands

Tip! Always be on the lookout for items you can use in your art center. One day my mom offered her beloved Tupperware to anyone who could possibly use it. I saw these little plates that held matching cups and immediately thought, "Art!" Mom was delighted that I could use her Tupperware—until she heard I was going to use it for paint! I explained that her plates would be well loved and well used in this unconventional manner. And indeed they have been! They are perfect paint palettes!

Tupperware plates used as paint palettes

ROLLERS AND RUBBER BRAYERS

Painting with rollers is a favorite with twos and threes. Rollers are fun to use, and there are so many choices available these days! Purchase as many different types as possible. If you rinse them after each use and store them carefully, they can last quite a long time.

Rollers come in a variety of sizes, shapes, and textures. Foam rollers are typical in early childhood classrooms, and they are inexpensive, but my personal favorites are small trim rollers (from the hardware store) and rubber brayers. Each type of roller produces a different textured effect, and you can feel the difference as you paint with them. Sample a variety of rollers to see what you like, and observe the children carefully to see where their interests lie.

Plastic microwave food containers, takeout food containers, or any other containers that are shallow and wide enough to accommodate the rollers work well to hold the paint for rolling. (Discount School Supply sells a four-paint roller tray that lasts for years.) Be sure to use a container that has a lip so the roller doesn't push out the paint. If you like, you can also use squirt bottles to squirt the paint directly onto the paper, canvas, or tray.

SPRAY PAINTING

To spray paint with twos and threes, use small spray bottles from your local dollar store, hardware store, or garden store. Any small-handled spray bottle will do.

Spray painting works best with water and liquid color. To make this type of spray paint, fill the bottle with water to one inch from the top. Next, add the desired amount of liquid watercolor paint or food coloring. Put the lid on and shake the bottle lightly. Alternatively, you could use water and a few tablespoons of tempera paint. With this type of paint, close the lid tightly and shake the bottle hard to blend the mixture thoroughly. This type of spray paint produces artwork that is more textured.

Spray painting is a big hit with young children! Following are a few tips for spray painting with young children:

- You can use spray paint indoors at the easel or on very large pieces of cardboard.

- Because it can be quite messy, most teachers prefer to do spray painting projects outdoors. Clip large paper (butcher paper or large easel paper) to a fence with clothespins, and then spray the paint. When the children are not using the spray bottles, turn the handles backward and hang them on the fence.

- Keep children a safe distance (at least three feet) apart, and make sure children don't spray one another, especially in the face. This is particularly a concern during warmer weather, when they may be tempted to use the paint to cool off. Use language that lets children know this is paint—not water—and must be used only where you designate.

- If you live in a cold climate, spray painting is a great incentive for getting outdoors in the winter. Spray paint in the snow!

- Store the paint bottles upright. If a bottle stops working, its nozzle is probably clogged. Try holding your finger over the nozzle for a few seconds while pumping the trigger to build pressure. When you remove your finger from the nozzle, it will release the extra pressure and clear the nozzle.

- For tempera spray paint, give the bottle a small shake periodically to keep the mixture well blended and flowing smoothly.

- Be aware that the children's hands will probably get paint on them. Liquid watercolor and food coloring may be difficult to clean off at first.

Watching the colors run

Spray painting outside

Painting with intention

TIRE PAINTING

Tire painting is a favorite painting activity among young children too. Many twos and threes love to play with toy vehicles, and they are doubly attracted to the idea of driving the little cars and trucks through puddles of paint.

Use shallow trays filled with thin layers of paint. Choose plastic toy cars and trucks. (Plastic ones are easier to wash than the metal ones.) Choose toy vehicles that have tires with a bit of tread on them so they make distinct tire marks. Offer different vehicle sizes and tire treads so children can explore the differences.

SPIN ART

In the old days, children could use a record player to spin a circle of paper while dripping paint onto it, creating an amazing, swirly artwork. Record players have gone the way of the dinosaur, but you can still make spin art in the classroom!

Using an ordinary salad spinner, children can produce the same effect. First take the lid off the salad spinner. Then lay a circle of paper in the bottom of the spinner. Next, have the child spoon or squirt paint onto the paper. You may want to limit the amount of paint; a few squirts or spoonfuls should do. If children overdo it, you can show them the excess paint pooling in the bottom of the spinner. Close the lid and let the child turn the crank or push the button to spin the salad spinner. As the spinner turns, it distributes the paint in beautiful patterns across the paper. After a minute or two of spinning, take the lid off and reveal the wonderful and colorful spin art!

Here are a few tips for doing spin art with twos and threes:

- Have only one child at a time doing this activity.

- Have several paper circles cut and ready in advance. Write each child's name on the back of a circle before creating the spin art.

- Try different-colored papers for different effects.

- Have three or four paint colors available for the children.

- Water down the paint slightly.

- Be aware that spin art can get messy. Tape a plastic grocery bag around the outside of the salad spinner's bowl to keep paint mess to a minimum.

Salad spinner art

EYEDROPPER PAINTING

Children can create eyedropper art on small paper, large paper, coffee filters, thick watercolor paper, or poster board. To paint with eyedroppers, use either liquid watercolor paint in bright colors or tempera paint diluted with water.

Learning to squeeze the eyedroppers takes some practice. Have the children get used to eyedroppers with water only, or with colored water and cornstarch at the sensory table. After a few successes, move the eyedroppers over to the art center and fill them with paint instead.

Eyedropper art

BUBBLE PAINTING AND BUBBLE PRINTING

To do bubble painting, add food coloring or liquid watercolor paint to a bubble solution. You can use store-bought bubble solution or make your own. (For a recipe, see appendix B.) Use a bubble wand to blow colored bubbles onto a large sheet of paper. As they land and pop, they will leave bubble-shaped marks in a variety of sizes and colors!

Bubble printing

Use pieces of bubble wrap to do bubble printing. If possible, find bubble wrap with bubbles in varying sizes. Tape the wrap to a table or a tray. Give the children rollers or brushes with assorted paints and let them paint directly onto the bubble wrap. Then have them lay a large sheet of paper on top of the painted bubble wrap and lift the paper to see the print. If you like, repeat the process the next day using the same paper to create a layered print.

ICE CUBE PAINTING

Ice cube painting offers a fun and entertaining project well suited for midyear or wintertime. It teaches some important science concepts as well! The ice cubes start out in solid form and begin melting during use, turning into liquid form, which provides an opportunity for simple conversation about the states of matter. As colors blend, children can learn about color mixing.

Ice cube painting

Fill a standard ice cube tray with water, and then add food coloring or liquid watercolor paints. The more color you add, the more vibrant the ice cube paints will be. Put the tray in the freezer for about sixty minutes or longer. Take the tray out and insert wooden craft sticks into the semifrozen cubes.

Finish freezing the cubes overnight. When you're ready to begin painting, take the ice cube paints out of the freezer and let them stand a few minutes. Place heavyweight paper in trays, and let the children paint!

Alternatively, you can freeze the paints in small paper cups. Simply peel off the paper cup to reveal the "paint pop." You can also use plastic molds to create Popsicle-shaped paint pops. Remind the children that these pops are not for eating!

Instead of using the water mixture, you could fill the ice cube trays, paper cups, or plastic molds with regular tempera paint. The resulting paint pops have a thick and creamy texture. Let the children explore and experiment with different textures and results. Be sure to have a camera and notepad ready to document the fun!

MONOPRINTING

This is a multisensory project that young children absolutely love! To begin this process, the children squirt the paint on a tray. They love to squeeze the bottle as hard as they can and exercise their muscles. Next, they roll out the paint with rubber brayers. Let the children explore and play in the paint and enjoy the sensory experience. They can scrape or draw in the paint however they like, using fingers, scrapers, craft sticks, and so on. When they are finished playing with the paint, help the chil-

dren lay their paper on the paint and pat the paper gently. Finally, have them lift the paper to expose a magnificent work of art! The first time children see their work, they are amazed!

Tip! **When you're using liquid watercolor paint, put newspaper under the paper to absorb excess liquid. Trays are also helpful.**

Rolling out the paint

Lifting the paper

Squirting paint onto trays

DRIP ART

The children can create drip art by using several squirt bottles filled with various colors of paint. They hold the bottles at the top of a piece of cardboard or poster board. They squeeze the bottles to let the colors drip down the cardboard, one color over another. They do not touch the paint. The outcome is long drips of layered colors that puddle at the bottom. Adults look at the finished product and think, "Wow! That's really cool!" But the excitement for children lies in the process of squeezing the paint and watching it ooze and pool.

You can do this activity using an easel or a large cardboard box placed on the floor or using tented cardboard on a table. Cover the floor or table with newspaper to catch the inevitable drips. Enjoy watching the process, hearing the giggles, and admiring the beautiful, colorful layered artwork!

Many people think two- and three-year-olds cannot paint still lifes. I have done it with older children, and one year I decided to try it with younger children. I gathered the plastic fruit from the dramatic play area (so children would know it was not being offered to eat) and placed the fruit on the art table. I invited the children to paint a picture of the fruit. Several children came over to paint right away. One child painted each fruit one by one. After she painted the fruits individually, she looked once more at the plate of fruit. She then painted a picture of the plate with all the fruit on it. I was fascinated by this process of observation and synthesis.

A dish full of plastic fruits

Drip art, standing

The finished products

An amazing two-year-old artist paints a still life.

Still lifes portraying each fruit

PAINTING WITH HANDS AND FEET

Fingerpainting is a perennial favorite with young children, unless they do not like getting their hands messy. Often even children who are sensitive to paint mess will fingerpaint anyway. They paint and then immediately wash up. Any paint can serve as fingerpaint, but fingerpaints designed for this use work the best. Strongly encourage the use of smocks for fingerpainting.

And let's not forget about painting with feet! Feet painting is exhilarating to children because it provides so much tactile input to their bodies! Feet painting needs continuous adult supervision—both for safety (the paint is slippery) and to contain the mess. Here are two methods you can use for feet painting:

- Have the child sit on a chair and lift one foot at a time. Paint the child's feet using whatever color the child wants. Help the child onto a large piece of paper to walk around and make footprints on it. Butcher paper works well.

- Put a thin layer of paint in each of a few trays on the ground. Hold the child's hands to help the child step into and out of the paint and then onto the paper. You must help the child, because the paint is slippery.

If you're nervous about mess, the first method offers more teacher control. Some children like the tickles of the paintbrush; others do not like it at all. The second method is usually the most enjoyable for children. This method gives them total control, and it has an element of risk, which makes it exciting.

It is best to do this project outdoors in warm weather. If you do it outside, have a garden hose ready for quick cleanup. You can do this project indoors as well. Have a bucket of warm soapy water and a towel ready so you can wash and dry feet immediately after painting.

Painting with fingers

Painting with fingers—and hands and arms!

Painting with feet

Making colorful footprints!

Collages

Young children love to make collages! They offer not only a sensory experience, but also the ability to keep adding to an artwork

Using squeezable glue bottles is great fun for young children, and it helps in developing fine-motor skills and strength. Early on, use the smallest (four-ounce) squeeze bottles and refill them often. Later you can build toward using larger (seven-ounce) squeeze bottles. You can also offer a container of glue with a glue brush, paintbrush, or rubber applicator. Both bottles and brushes offer children good opportunities to develop fine-motor skills and hand-eye coordination.

Here are a few tips for collage projects with young children:

- Items to use for collages include tissue paper, glitter, pom-poms, yarn, shiny paper, feathers, nature items, cellophane, felt, faux fur, sequins, yarn, foam pieces, crepe paper, pipe cleaners, string, ripped paper or paper scraps, recycled artwork cut into pieces, and other assorted items and craft materials.

- Have materials cut in advance. Sort the materials into sandwich bags or divided containers.

- When making collages with heavier items, such as nature items, or large amounts of materials, glue them onto poster board or cardboard. These boards will hold the weight of materials and glue better than paper will. Children of this age enjoy using as many materials in their collages as they possibly can!

- Tint the glue by adding food coloring, liquid watercolor paint, or tempera paint.

- Encourage children to cut or rip old artworks themselves to reuse for their collage work.

Young children need to experiment with materials.

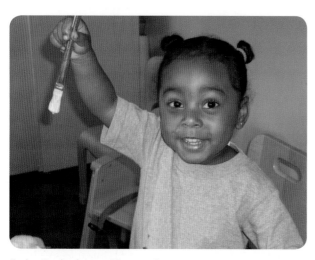

Exploration leads to positive experiences.

Supportive adults offer enthusiasm and encouragement.

Sculpture

Giving the children exposure to a variety of materials and artistic techniques opens their world to new experiences. Sculptures and multidimensional materials offer a new perspective on what art is and what can be created. Very often these projects are big and enjoyed thoroughly as group projects.

CLAY

Don't underestimate a two's or three's ability to use real clay, which offers an array of experiences for a young child in a tactile and creative way. Clay offers a much different experience than playdough. For early experiences with clay, it is best to limit the tools. Begin with a few basic playdough rollers and cutters. Provide an opportunity to manipulate the clay, and then discuss the differences between it and playdough.

Once children are comfortable using clay, perhaps during their second or third experience, provide real clay tools purchased from the art store. Giving children the opportunity to work with authentic materials exposes them to the true creative experience of an artist. The way the tools feel against the hard clay is a wonderful sensory experience. In fact, I have observed adults carving away and finding it very therapeutic!

Adding water changes the clay experience. Some younger children may not like the wet and slimy texture, but you will find many who simply love the silky feeling of the wet clay mixture on their hands—or arms for that matter!

A child's first experience with clay

Her second experience with clay, water added

Her third experience with clay. She is very comfortable!

Enjoying her third experience with clay. The camera captures a sequence showcasing her experience.

PAPIER-MÂCHÉ

Making papier-mâché is much easier than one might think. It can be a messy project, but children love it. A few different recipes for making papier-mâché are available. (See two you can try in appendix B.) Here is a simple papier-mâché project to create a sphere:

1. Cut or rip newspaper or other paper into strips.

2. Make the mixture.

3. Blow up and tie off the balloons.

4. Dip the paper strips into the papier-mâché mixture.

5. Make the wet paper strips adhere to the balloons.

6. Let the papier-mâché dry overnight or longer.

7. Paint the surface.

8. Allow the sculpture to dry and harden. It can then be cut if desired or left as is.

The possibilities are endless!

Tip! **Rip the paper instead of cutting it; it makes the process work more smoothly. Also, for this younger age group, I sometimes find the glue mixture recipe (rather than the flour mixture one) is easier for them to dip the paper into and is more appealing to them. A friend of mine taught our group to squeeze out the excess with their fingers, as shown in the second photo above.**

Making a chrysalis

Painting the mountains

BOX SCULPTURES

Making box sculptures is a favorite project for children. With tape and glue to bind them together, use a variety of boxes of assorted sizes and shapes to create a sculpture. You may want to plan ahead of time what the box sculpture will become, or you may want to simply enjoy the process of spontaneously creating it together! Typically, this activity will take days to work on and complete.

A group box sculpture consists of layers and layers of creations. Often the younger children enjoy

Getting started

reapplying materials over their existing work. If a child wants a portion to be saved, then you should protect and respect that portion as much as possible. One idea could be covering the area to be saved with paper.

Children love to create, especially when there are materials on hand, readily available for them to use. Have a box of recycled items, such as paper towel tubes, small boxes (the size of pudding or granola bars), and egg cartons, handy for whenever a quick project is needed. A roll of masking tape can be kept right in the box for quick access as well.

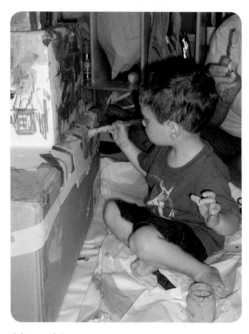

A box sculpture

The most wonderful thing about doing a group box sculpture is that it is a child-led community-building activity. It gives children the opportunity to make decisions about how to paint and design the project. A group box sculpture is also a good opportunity to help children develop their understanding of what it means to work together: to creatively and cohesively decide on how to work together and how to gain a mutual understanding. It's possible that your group box sculpture will start off in one direction and end up as something totally different—which is half the fun!

Example One: House Sculpture

When doing a theme unit about families, we decided to make a classroom house. The project started with one big box, several smaller boxes, and paper towel tubes. The project took several days. On day one, we built the structure. We started with several colors of masking tape and glue. The children went straight for the tape and began taping right onto the boxes. They then began connecting the boxes, which was a good starting point to get the children involved as a group and to make the structure stable. As it got bigger and more elaborate, an adult stood by, ready to help as needed. It was amazing to hear the children's language while observing them and to watch their plans unfold throughout the entire process. That evening, I retaped any loose parts and added glue for strength, knowing the next stage of building was approaching.

Day two consisted of painting. We offered the children a variety of paints, brushes, and rollers and allowed them to paint as they desired. On day three, we offered the children the tape again and Cray-Pas. By now, of course, they had taken complete ownership of the project. Some children had their own ideas about what to add, and others just plain enjoyed adding their parts while exploring the materials. One child discovered while coloring the sides of the box that the walls needed "wallpaper" and asked for paper. What a great idea! I gave her paper, and she colored it and then taped it to the side of the house sculpture.

Then, for another two days the house sculpture and the remaining materials were available for those still interested to continue working on it. Finally, I cut out photos of each child and placed them on the outside of the house sculpture, completing our classroom community! Documentation panels were created with the children's language and their photos taken during the house-sculpture-making process, and these were hung over the house sculpture for the families to enjoy. It was a great beginning project!

Busy workers!

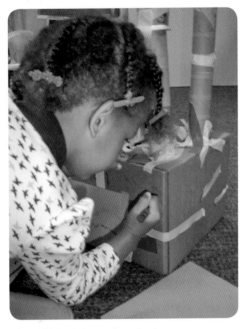

One child decided to make wallpaper.

created an array of language opportunities and scientific exploration as we began guessing what paint colors to mix to make the ones we wanted. As children began decorating the upper areas of the house, one little girl declared, "It's the bedroom!" as she decorated the peak of the house. Another child painted doors and windows on the house. As you can see in the photos below, the work area was *not* neat and tidy. They show a very child-centered and exciting workspace, one filled with creative explorations. The gingerbread house became a project filled with compromise, sharing, and rich-language conversation among the children.

Example one: A house sculpture

Example two: A gingerbread house

Example Two: Gingerbread House

Jan Brett's beloved children's book *Gingerbread Baby* was the inspiration for our next box sculpture. We began with two box houses to paint, but the children quickly focused on only one of those houses. Day one was spent painting the house white. On day two, a roof was added, and the children used pastel-colored paints to decorate. On day three, we brought out collage materials for them to use in decorating the gingerbread house.

Many exciting ideas were generated. Some of the children thought pom-poms, sequins, and pipe cleaners resembled the candies pictured in the storybook. Two children wanted more colors, which

Example Three: Three Bears' Beds

During "Goldilocks and the Three Bears" units, I often have the children make large bed sculptures. The beds are often made from thick, flat pieces of cardboard. On day one, make Papa Bear's bed (too hard), using paint and glitter. On day two, make Mama Bear's bed (too soft), using packing pillows, pom-poms, feathers, or similar materials with colored glue. On day three, make Baby Bear's bed (just right), using felt, fur, and soft items with colored glue. The children have a great time with this activity.

A "bed" for Mama Bear

Example Four: Miscellaneous Box and Cardboard Sculptures

Sometimes wonderful and spontaneous child-inspired art is the best! A plan is not essential. Simply put out the materials and watch the creativity and excitement begin! For instance, offer the children a flat box, along with cardboard tubes, masking tape, colored tape, and colored glue with brushes. On the second and third days, put out squeeze bottles full of glue and more tape and see what happens!

LARGE SHEETS OF CARDBOARD

Large sheets or pieces of cardboard make an excellent canvas for painting or other various projects. The best part is they are free! You could put a large flat sheet of cardboard on a tabletop, against an easel, or along a fence. Another idea is to use large sheets from a cardboard box not yet cut down. We did this project during our construction unit while the "workers" were learning about the job of carpenters and painting a wall. It was a three-day project. We cut out one side of the large box, leaving a trifold structure that could stand on its own. The children were able to paint it using big brushes and rollers. They began to have their own ideas and added crayons and carpenter pencils.

Large cardboard painting with rubber brayers

Rollers on large cardboard

Large and thin boxes taped shut make excellent canvas material. First paint them white to give a clean slate and fresh start. When the paint is completely dry, put the boxes out for the children to paint as desired!

Extra-large boxes (such as appliance boxes) can be first used for play. There is nothing children love more than boxes to climb in and out of! You can then cut windows and doors into the box, or tape a few boxes together to create specific play items: a house, a boat, a car, a school bus, or a carriage. The children can then paint the boxes to represent the imaginary item and use it in dramatic play.

EGGSHELL SCULPTURES

During a unit of nursery rhymes, the children created eggshell sculptures. To have small bits and pieces ready for sculpting, crunch up all of the eggshells in advance, or you can let the children crunch the shells for that sensory feeling, which many enjoy. In fact, for many children this project is much more about the sensory experience of exploring both the eggshells and the glue than it is about creating a sculpture.

Tinted eggshells and glue on foil

Exploring eggshells and glue with fingers

Eggshells and tinted glue on paper

The children were able to use as many eggshell pieces as they wanted, and they had their choice of using either a squeeze bottle of glue or a brush and container. Some children noticed if they mixed the glue and eggshells together, a different texture resulted and their sculpture took on a different effect. Some children loved the sticky glue on their hands and some did not; these children avoided touching the gluey sculpture as they created it and immediately washed their hands. Either direction is perfectly fine. If you allow the children to use excessive amounts of glue, it is best to have a sturdy base underneath: strong pieces of cardboard or poster board work nicely. We tinted our eggshells green, but whether you color the shells is a personal choice.

GIANT PANCAKES

Giant sculptures are a fun and unique project to try. The children make a sculpture that imitates something familiar that they can associate with—yet it is *so big*! A friend's discovery of artist Claes Oldenburg's work (a sculptor who creates large-scale food sculptures) inspired a project the children absolutely love! It is fun and provides several days' worth of artistic and creative adventure!

Large circle shapes that looked like round paper pillowcases were purchased from Oriental Trading Company. We filled the giant circles with crumpled newspaper and then taped them shut to keep them full. On the first day, the children painted the stuffed circles using rollers and brushes and yellow and brown paints of assorted textures. It was an explorative experience as the children figured out how to paint what they thought a big pancake would look like.

Squeezing on the "syrup"

The next day, the pancakes were put out again, as were different brushes and different shades of yellow, brown, and orange paints. We created "butter" from cereal boxes: we taped the cereal boxes closed, and the children painted the boxes yellow using paint brushes and rollers. When they were dry, we attached the cereal boxes to the top of the pancakes. On the third day, we brought out the squirt bottles and filled them with thinned-out paint to make "syrup." This was the moment the children anticipated the most, because they love using the squirt bottles and thought squeezing "syrup" would be fun. One child requested sparkles, so we brought out the glitter too.

The children loved this project! One of our large pancake sculptures was later placed in the school lobby for children and parents to view. It was also placed in our art exhibit.

SIMPLE WOODWORKING

Younger children enjoy making wood sculptures using assorted small pieces of wood and glue. Squeeze-bottle glue and brushed-on glue both work well. While the sculptures are drying, it is a good idea to add a dab or two of wood glue, if necessary, to open areas or cracks in the sculptures to hold them together more strongly—but be careful not to dismantle the child's work. A wood-sculpture project can last several days. The children could

Painting a giant "pancake"

even add a layer or two of paint to the sculpture or add other items that interest them. Placing the sculpture on a tray covered with a layer of wax paper is a good way to store the project and continue the work each day. If trays are not available, cut cardboard also could be used.

Simple woodworking

The Progression Stages of Using Scissors

Teaching two- and three-year-olds to use scissors is easier than you might think, for children typically learn to use them successfully in no time at all. The learning is a simple progression that begins with playdough and playdough scissors. Once the child understands how to cut playdough with the playdough scissors, move to cutting paper with the playdough scissors; they are sharp enough to cut paper but not sharp enough to cut hair or the child's fingers. Once you've helped the child learn to manipulate the playdough scissors and coordinate his fingers properly, you can switch to safety scissors, which are a little sharper. Finally, you can bring out the rounded-tip scissors. It is a personal

Learning to use scissors

preference of mine never to use pointed-tip scissors in my classroom. The pointed-tip scissors can be dangerous and could lead to the child cutting his skin, poking his eye, or injuring the child beside him.

Using scissors builds fine-muscle strength and develops pre-writing skills and fine-motor skills. In addition, I have found that having "cutting bins" full of scrap paper, strips of paper, crepe paper, strips of wallpaper samples, and so on available to children who need focus or as an activity for a short period of time works great.

Step one: Playdough with playdough scissors

Take Art Outdoors!

Art experiences outdoors are exciting and often bigger and better than those indoors. Anything you can do artistically inside, you can do outside, only bigger, better, and more! Children can express themselves freely with big movements and an excess of materials. For adults, taking art outdoors means less worry about messy materials and creating a messy room. Often materials such as paint can be easily washed off or hosed clean. When the teachers are more accepting of this form of art and more freedom is given to the children, the children become more apt to explore and create openly.

Step two: Paper with playough scissors

Roller painting at the fence

Step three: Using safety scissors

Step four: Using rounded-tip scissors

Watercolors, sunshine, and shadows

Art outdoors changes the experience.

Layering and Revisiting Previous Work

Younger children learn best through hands-on experiences. This often includes revisiting previous work, repeating techniques, or trying something different. There is great benefit to allowing children to explore and to explore some more.

Layering work involves bringing out an old project and adding a new dimension. For any layering activity, the first layer is paint. The layering can continue using more paint, as well as adding other materials and mediums of art production. For example, on the first day, the project could begin with darker shades of paint and rollers. The second day could bring lighter tints of paint and brushes, possibly even thinner brushes. And further yet, the third day could bring oil pastels colored on top. Numerous possibilities exist! You can try many techniques, chosen either by you or by the children themselves. Work can last for weeks this way. Sometimes you might chose to put the work away and bring it back out after several days or weeks. Should you choose to give them a fresh start, painting on a base color creates a clean canvas. You could then add textures, paints, glue, and assorted materials. The possibilities are endless! In my experience, the more you and the children experiment with this, the more ideas you will develop.

Displaying Children's Art

Displaying children's art is very important. It should be displayed year-round. Try to hang artwork at two heights: low, so children can easily see it, and high, so adults can easily read any documentation panels that may be included. Present a diversity of paintings, drawings, photos, and language. Hang the work on the classroom walls or on bulletin boards.

Here are some tips for displaying art in the classroom:

- If using a bulletin board, keep the backing simple and without designs. A solid color will accent the children's work without becoming distracting.

- Consider using a backing of fabric instead of paper, as the fabric will last all year (or longer) and won't fade or show staple holes.

- Don't overcrowd the artwork.

- Trim artwork only if necessary. Be certain not to disturb the child's actual work, for instance, by cutting their work into a shape to fit a theme.

- Borders are fine as long as they do not distract from the children's work. Simple is best.

- Mounting children's work gives definition and adds beauty. I often use black poster board cut in half as a year-long mounting for each child's work throughout the year. It holds twelve-by-eighteen-inch paper, and you can secure a label at the bottom with the child's name typed on.

- Children's language about their work can be added, as well as teacher dictation about the process and the emotions of the child during the experience.

- Adding photos of the children taken while they are working on the art really captures the true experience.

Respect the child who does not want to participate in the art center. I have worked in classrooms where teachers force every child to make a particular project, in order to be certain every child has one hanging on the wall. Despite good intentions, it is not appropriate to force a child to participate in the art center if he is not interested. To take pressure off the child who does not want to participate (and even the child's parent), I often do not label artwork that is hanging on the wall or bulletin board. And typically I display more collaborative art projects than individual pieces in my classroom.

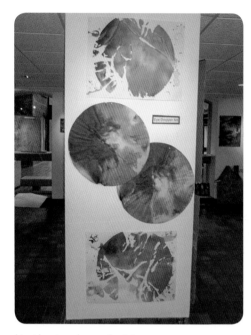

Liquid watercolors and paints

Monoprinting in hallway with photo documentation

GROUP DISPLAYS AND ART EXHIBITS

Explore different ideas when showing and sharing the children's art. Depending on your time, space, and motivation, group displays can be small, only a few pieces, or very big, requiring a whole room! During conference times, display artwork in the classroom, halls, or lobby. Maybe your school has an extra room, library, or other place to set up an art exhibit. Displaying the children's artwork as a group shows the world the true artists you have.

For the past few years, I have been fortunate to have had the opportunity to organize an art exhibit where I currently work. It was truly one of the most moving experiences I have ever had with art. I want to share my art exhibit experience simply to show you how magnificent young children's art truly can be when it is presented in a professional manner.

Individual panels in an art show

Exhibiting the art brings new meaning and respect to the children's work.

I collected the artwork throughout the year. I filed it, documented it, and took thousands of pictures. (Digital cameras are the best invention!) I secured the art gallery and set up the artwork. The exhibit consisted of mostly large group pieces placed throughout the gallery that highlighted a variety of artistic techniques the children had learned and worked on all year. I also included many of the variations of the art projects, as well as the experiences that had been modified and explored. I wanted the artwork to represent the children as a group, as a community of young people who worked together on a year-long creative journey. I included photos and documentation panels that shared the children's efforts, conversation, and decision making. The photos and documentation also related the children's struggles and explorations.

In addition to the group artwork, each child had her own panel consisting of several smaller pieces of independent work. One year two children had small photography exhibits because they had expressed particular interest in learning to take photographs—and they really learned to take great shots! It was an amazing experience.

Over my career, I have worked in various environments, including family child care settings, where space for displaying artwork was very limited. I have now learned to think big and to search for resources. You never know what will be available in your community, and I encourage you to go explore.

If you choose to save a lot of the children's work for conferences, art shows, or other times, showing artwork in bulk requires first saving the work in an organized fashion.

Archiving and Creating Portfolios

Saving children's work takes diligence, space, and organization. It really is a lot of work to hold on to artwork and keep up with the documentation and storage necessary. Here are some tips for making it work:

- Start your documentation and individual files for children in the beginning of the year, and follow through all year. Setting aside a time, weekly or biweekly, is most helpful.

- Have a designated space for all children's work before it gets separated. Large boxes, sections of a large drying rack, or two sheets of poster board taped together work well. Place all items (with names and dates) in the designated space. This will keep items safe and protect artwork from getting bent until you have time to sort through it all.

- Have a separate filing system for each child.

Using portfolios for children is a great way to keep art and drawings, track development, hold teacher notes, and combine photos and language dictation. The portfolio is developed in the beginning of the year and then added to throughout the year. Ideas for portfolios include the following:

- Diaries: Include children's language dictation, photos, art, and written work. You could use composition notebooks, binders, and plastic sleeves. The diary could be a summary of the child's experiences and works within the program.

- Books: Art that is collected throughout the year could be turned into a stunning art portfolio collection for the child to take home at the end of the year. The book could start from the beginning of the year and showcase all the artwork, the child's progression, and photos and language dictation from the child. Such books are quite a keepsake!

- Share portfolios at conferences, and then give them to parents at the end of the year.

Every year, parents tell me how much they love their child's art, and how they would love to save it all, but there is simply *so much*! I surely understand this feeling toward a child's beloved artwork, so I offer some suggestions to share with parents:

- Save the child's work in a book, box, or large bin with a lid.

- Display artwork on walls.

- Frame individual pieces.

- Make artwork into notebook covers or inserts.

- Use paintings as wrapping paper.

- Cut some pieces up to make note cards, thank-you cards, invitations, calendars, diaries or journals, or cookbook covers.

- Give them as special gifts (laminated or framed); add a photo and a drawing or message to make it personal.

- Archive the artwork in binders. If the art is too big to fit in the binder, photograph it and place the photo in the binder instead. Also, photograph all the artwork, and use your computer to create a digital portfolio or gallery.

the back of the artwork so I don't disrupt the child's work. If I am in a hurry, I attach a sticky note with the information I do not have time to dictate in that moment.

Marking the date a piece was created is very important. It allows you to chart the child's development throughout the year, as well as to know and to understand where that child is developmentally at any given time. Children go through a tremendous developmental and emotional growth period when they are two and three. Observing their development is crucial!

Writing on Children's Artwork

Writing on children's artwork is a topic that can generate mixed feelings. Writing a child's name on her artwork is something we all just do in a hurry throughout our busy day. Until about five years ago, I did not think about it too much. One day I sent a piece of artwork home with a child. The child's mother asked to speak with me the next morning. She asked if I could please stop writing on the front of her artwork, as she felt her daughter's work to be so lovely that she wanted to frame some pieces.

From that moment on, I began to rethink my practice of writing on the front of children's artwork. I began to really consider it on a bigger level. Yes, her work was amazing, just as every other piece the children in the group made was amazing. And when we mark on the paper in any way, we alter their work, even in the slightest way. "How might I feel if someone wrote on my work," I wondered? In addition, I began to look at all of the artwork currently in the classroom. Several pieces had names written sloppily. On one piece, the child's name was spelled wrong and scribbled over the top. What does this say about the value of the child's work? Does it suggest it is not worthy of neat, tidy, well-thought-out marking? I now carefully put the name of the child and the date the piece was created on

Final Thoughts on Art

Art is an important element in a twos-and-threes program. It is critical to provide well-thought-out projects. When planning and facilitating projects, adults need to operate at their comfort level, but eventually all art projects being offered to children should be child led and process oriented. Because big messes are a concern of many adults, finding a balance is important to make the most of the experience.

We offer and explain art projects during our gathering circles. While the project typically starts as my idea, the children add their thoughts, and often the project changes and goes in a new direction because of their creative input. Sometimes we try ideas that just don't go very well. But they are great teachable moments and lead to further discovery. Having a camera and pencil and paper or sticky notes handy is very important; recording children's language and input goes best when you are prepared. I always jot down the communication, creative ideas, and problem solving that emerges at the art center.

When we are mindful of our offering of process, observations, and documentation, as well as the language we use with them, our self-reflection, and our presentation of their creative endeavors, we show children respect. Be flexible and allow children the freedom to explore and be spontaneous.

Celebrate all of the children's encounters and endeavors with art. Find the joy and wonder along the way—for the children, as well as ourselves! It is easy to create wonderful and stimulating art experiences for children. You are providing an early love of art and fostering creative art experiences to last a lifetime! I tell my children, "You are the artist. You decide how you want to create your work!"

When I set out the long brushes, they reminded this child of splatter painting, which of course led to him trying it out!

This child decided he needed more paint, so he went and got it.

He then decided to do monoprints!

The scraper on the foil left smooth tracks, which made this child think of a road, so she got a truck to make truck prints.

CHAPTER 4

Writing Exploration

Why is the writing table important and special for this age group? It is a place where young children develop writing skills, reading skills, vocabulary, communication skills, fine-muscle control, creativity, imagination, memory, and critical thinking. Simple, scribbly lines and circles soon take on shape and meaning. These scribbles are the foundation for writing letters and creating more complex drawings.

Facilitating Writing

When younger children visit the writing table, they tend to offer more ideas and language with the help of a facilitating adult. The role of the adult in this situation is as a guide, offering choices. The adult should note the children's interests, such as preferred materials and what they are thinking about. The adult should have a pencil or pen in hand ready for dictation and for taking notes about the child in the moment. Here is an example of how a teacher might guide a student and of the notes taken:

Teacher: "Tyrone, I see you have decided to come to the writing table! I am so glad! We have many colors today. Which do you think you will choose first?"

Tyrone: "Green!"

Teacher: "Green? Excellent! What do you think you might draw today?"

Teacher notes: 09/15—Tyrone came to the writing table for the first time. He independently chose green. He did not offer a reason for that choice. He scribbled and made large strokes across the paper. Next, he took the blue crayon and colored on top of the green. Language was limited during his time at the table. Teacher offered him stickers, which he accepted. He needed help to peel them and placed two on his picture. Then he stated, "Done!" and left the area.

This type of facilitation is not always possible during a busy day. But do try to do this early in the year to help you get to know the children, and keep trying sporadically throughout the year to observe development and take notes for family conferences. As the year progresses and children learn what to expect from the adult, they will offer ideas and thoughts more readily.

It is important not to push a child who is not ready or willing to offer language. It's equally important to avoid leading their language or drawing too much. Adults should be present for children who wish to write or draw, but they shouldn't draw or write with them. While sitting at the writing table, adults may be tempted to doodle or to draw *for* children. But this interferes with the development of younger children's ability to freely express themselves.

Here are some constructive questions and comments an adult can use at the writing table:

- "I see you are using (color)."

- "I notice you are covering the page completely! Wow!"

- "You sure are working hard on this picture!"

- "Would you like to tell me about your picture?"

- "Is there a message you want me to write on your picture?"

- "Is there anything else you need for your picture?"

- "Tell me about your drawing!"

- "Is there anything else you would like to say about your picture?"

- "Should I write anything else for your picture?"

Avoid comments like these:

- "What a pretty picture!"

- "What's that?"

- "Is that a rainbow?"

- "Wow! That's pretty!"

- "I love it!"

Tip: Write dictations in quotation marks on the *back* of a child's work. You could also use a separate piece of paper and tape it onto the back. Sometimes the latter strategy is helpful if multiple children are at the writing table and you are taking multiple notes at once, if the messages are longer, or if the child is making several dictations.

In addition to facilitating at the writing table, teachers must also encourage children to visit it. The trick is finding ways to keep them coming over as a choice. Children at this age are often busy, so we need to find ways to grab their attention. Here are some ideas:

- Keep the area clutter-free, comfortable, and inviting.

- Make the writing table aesthetically pleasing and eye catching.

- Change materials often to refresh children's interest.

- Know the children and their varied interests. Provide materials that suit those interests, such as specific colors, themed stickers, and so on.

- Be available and attentive.

- Be willing to get something for use in the writing center (such as extra stickers or tape) if a child asks for it.

- Try new ideas! Trying something completely different often inspires the children's curiosity.

Expand the writing center opportunities as the children become comfortable and are developmentally ready for new activities. In my classroom, for example, the year begins very simply. Offerings are repetitious for a few weeks while I get to know the children. Usually I set out simple paper, crayons, colored pencils, and chalk. Once I understand the abilities, temperaments, and interests in the classroom, I expand the choices offered.

Writing Media

Having a variety of writing media at the writing table keeps it novel and exciting. It also gives the children exposure to a variety of experiences. This age group is far more capable with different writing utensils than you might think!

Offering a variety of writing media is very beneficial for children. Each implement offers a different writing feel, a different texture, a different color, and a different effect on the paper. Variety will keep children returning to the area, knowing they will constantly have new choices. You will find that children will ask for specific materials when they know what is available and what is frequently offered.

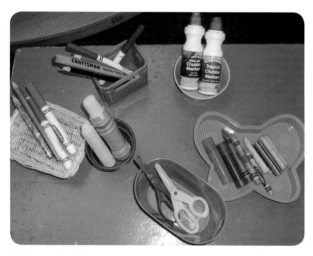

Writing table materials

A more sophisticated table with clipboards, authentic writing materials, and tape

Consider offering thick crayons, thin crayons, glitter crayons, rainbow crayons (pastel and regular), thick colored pencils, thin colored pencils, carpenter pencils, regular pencils with erasers, and large pencils with erasers. Some other ideas include thick markers, thin markers, sidewalk chalk, thin chalk, oil pastels, charcoal pencils, watercolor pencils, silky twist-up crayons, and pens.

Tip! **For this age group, use chalk holders to prevent chalk breakage. Great chalk holders are available for both small chalk and sidewalk chalk. I got my sidewalk chalk holders from Discount School Supply and my smaller holders from Parent-Teacher Supply. Sometimes I leave the natural chalk out (without holders) so the children can feel the texture of the chalk.**

Writing Surfaces

The materials on which children write are just as important as the writing utensils. Offering a variety of paper types and other writing surfaces is a simple way to bring children to the table. Variety gives the children choices and helps them develop their writing tastes.

Here are some different kinds of paper you might offer: construction paper, copy paper, old computer paper, lined paper, recycled paper, newspaper, small notepads, index cards, sticky notes, restaurant order pads, homemade booklets, new and used envelopes, scrap paper, crepe paper, paper strips, paint color samples, drawing paper, and watercolor paper.

A drawing pad and authentic art materials

In addition to papers that come in small sizes, consider offering papers that cover the full surface of the writing table:

- Large butcher paper: This is a great way to cover the table, and it totally changes the way children use the writing table. It invites group collaboration and offers full–arm muscle opportunities. Butcher paper can become a layering space for a multiday project.

- Poster board: Poster board can be used as a one-day project or a multiday project. For example, children might paint on the poster board the first day and use drawing implements on the second day.

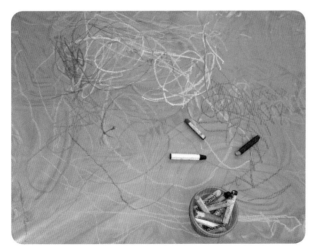

Poster board with a layer of paint and a layer of oil pastels

- Drafting paper: This is large paper recycled from architectural plans. Drawings and blueprints are on one side, and the reverse is blank. It makes a good surface for layered writing and drawing. Always be on the lookout for recycled materials to use, and ask parents if they can supply you with interesting and useful items.

Drafting paper, a ruler, and a pencil

Drafting paper

- Cardboard: Cardboard is a useful material at the writing table, as well as in art. Different types and thicknesses of cardboard materials can be used in a variety of ways. Cardboard is sturdy and can withstand thick or layered application of materials. Several children can work on cardboard over the course of a day or several days.

Tip! **Providing different-size papers has its benefits. Early on, it is important to have large writing surfaces for younger children. But as the year progresses, you can move toward smaller pieces of paper. You might change paper sizes simply for a change of pace or for specific purposes, such as making books, booklets, or note cards.**

You can also offer other nonpaper surfaces:

- Chalkboards: These can come in miniature, tabletop, and large sizes. Offer them with chalk and erasers.

- Whiteboards: Whiteboards are available in miniature, tabletop, and large sizes too. Offer them with damp sponges, dry paper towels or cloths, and nontoxic erasable markers.

- Real art canvas: Art canvas can be placed at the writing table too. After painting a canvas, the children can use oil pastels to draw or write on it.

- Clipboards: These are available in small and regular sizes. You can tie pencils onto the clipboards if you like. Clipboards are great for all-around classroom use as well. You can place them in the science center, dramatic play area, outdoors, or wherever children would like to use them. You will find that children begin to use them simply while walking around, just as they see adults taking notes!

A clipboard with a pencil attached by string

Other items to add:

- scissors

- glue sticks

- rulers

- stickers in assorted sizes and designs

- rubber or foam stampers with ink pads

Ink stamping on paper

Tape

Tape is a fabulous thing to offer to children! They enjoy using tape to embellish their artwork or writing projects with small scraps of paper they've ripped, torn, or cut. They also enjoy simply putting the tape on their papers or layering the tape—one piece over another!

At the beginning of the school year, wait a few weeks before you offer tape. First take a bit of time to get to know the children, build relationships, and understand how the environment is working for the current group. Add new materials slowly.

Masking tape is a wonderful start. Young children are particularly fond of the colored type. Early in the year, children will need help with the tape. A good method is ripping several pieces, or several colors, and having them ready for children to use as needed. If you are sitting at the writing table, it is easy to keep up with ripping new tape according to the desires of the children at the table. As time goes on and their skills grow, they will learn to rip the tape or cut the tape independently.

Rolls of tape readily available

Transparent tape takes longer to master. It is more difficult for children to manage. But again, the more practice young children have with it, the quicker they will gain the skills they need to use it independently.

Be prepared for children to use a lot of tape—especially at first. It takes time for them to understand how to use tape without getting pieces stuck together and twisted. With practice, they will master this skill. Letting children use tape freely allows them a wide range of opportunities to create masterpieces at both the writing table and in art projects.

Displaying Children's Work

Displaying children's writing and drawing is important. It shows them that their creative self-expressions have meaning and are valuable. Children are proud to see their work displayed for their family members and peers. When displayed in a professional way, their work is stunning—no matter where each child is developmentally.

Children's writing and drawings on display in an art gallery

Following are some tips for displaying children's writing and drawing work:

- Trim the borders of the writing or drawing to make the work even, centered, and smooth-edged.

- Mount the work on a piece of colored paper, black paper, poster board, or cardboard.

- Neatly print or type the child's message or quote in quotation marks on the backing paper underneath the drawing or writing, along with the child's name and the date.

- Add a photo of the child working on the writing or drawing.

Tip **Saving children's writing and drawing work is important. (See pages 68–69 for archiving ideas.) It takes time to develop archiving into your daily practice, but it's well worth the effort and is easy once you've gotten in the habit.**

A clutter-free, inviting writing center

Final Thoughts on the Writing Center

Adults often overlook writing activities for twos and threes because we don't always understand how to interpret their early scribbles or we are worried about supervising such young children with writing tools. It's true: your classroom may be the first exposure some children have to pencils, markers, and other implements. This makes your writing center—and your role as teacher—particularly important. How teachers present the area, the materials we offer, our presence with children, and how we display their work are crucial to their interest in writing and their development of skills.

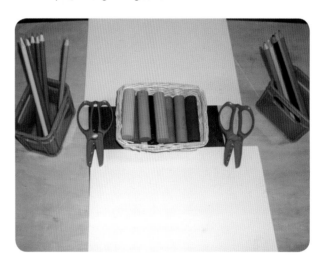

Remember to supply a variety of writing tools.

CHAPTER 5

Science and Nature

Two- and three-year-olds respond enthusiastically to science and nature activities. Including these in your curriculum is an important way to aid young children's discovery of and learning about their world. From observing rocks and moss with a magnifying glass to simply jumping in a mud puddle, science and nature activities are rich with meaningful discoveries and learning.

Your Role

As teachers and caregivers, we need to understand that our attitudes toward science and nature strongly affect children's experiences. If we approach science and nature with excitement and enthusiasm, we entice children with our words, tone, and body language. We build trust and interest. If we show fear, uncertainty, or disgust, then the children will assume that science and nature experiences are dangerous, unpleasant, and scary.

As in all other curriculum areas, in science and nature we should be facilitators, guides, and supportive mentors. We must offer children op-

portunities to explore, investigate, and inquire—unhindered by our own baggage. We should help children find joy, excitement, mystery, and knowledge in the natural world, in all living creatures, and in all weather conditions.

One great way to encourage inquiry is to admit what you don't know. Don't pretend to know it all with children. When children ask a question you can't answer, admit it—and offer to look up the information or ask someone who might know the answer. This simple act encourages children to be inquisitive and stokes their desire to learn more. When you say, "I like your question; let's look for an answer together," you confirm the value of questioning. As the year progresses, you might change your response to: "Hmm, what do you think? Where do you think we can find the answer?"

Here's some more language you can use to encourage inquiry:

- "I wonder..."

- "That's a great question. I think it could be..."

- "That's a great question. I wonder if it could be..."

- "I like the way you are thinking!"

- "I am not certain—let's find that information!"

- "Wow, that is really interesting! Why do you think that is?"

- "What do you think about that?"

- "Good eye spy!"

- "Great ear spy!"

- "Let's get a magnifying glass and look closer!"

These are just a few examples. You will find that as you practice using such encouraging language, your repertoire of phrases and questions will grow—and the children's repertoire will begin to grow as well. They will understand that their questions are important and interesting and can lead them to learn more about the world.

A simple moment in nature

Encourage children to use their senses.

THE EFFECT OF CHILDHOOD EXPOSURE TO NATURE

For my master's thesis, I studied and wrote about children's experiences in the natural world. I set out to learn if and how children's nature experiences have changed over the years. I learned a lot about educators' childhood experiences and how these affect the experiences they provide for children today. I interviewed educators in their twenties through their sixties. The evidence clearly showed the following:

- Everyone older than thirty was told each day as a child to go out and play—and be back home for lunch or dinner.

- All of the participants younger than thirty had no such freedom to roam.

- Educators' experiences—or lack of experiences—with the natural world played a key role in the attitudes and involvement they shared with children. Many over-thirties spoke fondly of their childhood experiences and believed that simple free play and time outdoors were very important for young children. Many under-thirties felt less passionate about the importance of time outdoors, and they mentioned disliking bugs and uncomfortable temperatures.

The experiences teachers had as children were embedded in their understanding of the world and their teaching practice. Those experiences defined how they lived their lives and how they interacted with children in the natural world. Such interactions directly affect the young children in their care. So on the children's behalf, we need to reflect on our practice, philosophies, and engagements with the natural world.

Admittedly, my survey involved just a handful of women in one geographical area. Although I do think it provided some important information, I don't think its findings hold true for everyone in a particular generation. I am certain there are many older and younger teachers alike who know the importance of getting children outdoors and do a wonderful job of exposing children to the natural world. In fact, I was thrilled when, right around the time I began my thesis, a big movement to get children outdoors began. This movement will be very beneficial to children now and in the future!

Children exploring a natural area

Take time to smell the flowers.

Science Center

A science center offers children the opportunity for a variety of science experiences. As children explore the items and activities in the science center, they discover the world around them. Science discoveries begin with simple experiences and grow with adult facilitation and the children's own interest.

When you facilitate in the science center, it is important to pose questions and to let children answer—and to encourage children to ask their own questions. Be sure to take photos and document the children's words and actions.

The items in the science center should allow children to see, touch, smell, or listen. Here are some important items to consider providing:

- magnifying glasses

- bug catchers (especially ones with magnifying-lens tops)

- large magnets or magnet wands (not magnet marbles or other small magnets)

- photos of nature items or phenomena that cannot be brought indoors or preserved, such as a tree, a river, a puddle, the sky, snow, fresh flowers, leaves of different colors, varied insects, and so on

- paper and pencils

- baskets to collect items that children find

- nature items such as pinecones, stones, tree bark, insects found dead, rocks, leaves, feathers, and shells

A science exploration shelf

Taking a closer look

- plants (ones children can help care for)

- weight scale

- color paddles (small plastic color panels available at school supply stores)

- color bottles (Mix water, food coloring, cooking oil, and glitter or sequins in a small transparent bottle. Hot-glue the lid on and tape it with masking tape too.)

- prisms

You don't have to have a large space to create a science center. Nor does it have to be a permanent installation. If your group includes very young children who mouth objects, or if you have a family child care with babies, you could have a portable science center (housed in a bin or box or on a large tray) that you can lift up and down as needed.

Tip! When I had a family child care with a multi-age group of children, I used a clear plastic over-the-door shoe holder as a portable science center. In each pocket, I placed interesting items that were safe for the children who could reach them.

A portable science center

When possible, it is great to have a shelf to hold science items and a nearby table so children can take the items off the shelf and use the table to explore them. Or instead of a shelf, you could use a bin with multiple compartments or a plastic food-serving container divided into several sections.

Caring for Plants

Caring for plants both indoors and out offers opportunities for children to learn about the life cycles of plants. Children also learn important lessons about caring for and respecting living things.

Give children a role in caring for plants.

HOUSEPLANTS

Green houseplants and flowering plants offer children the opportunity to provide ongoing care. You could start your year with one or two plants then add more as the year progresses. Be sure the plants you choose are not poisonous.

Letting children care for and water the plants is essential. Children can use spray bottles, small watering cans, small cups, or eyedroppers to water them. Containers that limit watering to small portions work best. Eyedroppers are great for preventing overwatering. Provide an eyedropper alongside a small container or baby food jar filled with water. This gives the children the ability to water whenever they want without watering too much! Use a tray under each plant to catch spills.

SEEDS AND SEEDLINGS

Starting seeds and transplanting seedlings is a great project for young children. Many scientific discoveries await children throughout the process. Children can see firsthand how a seed sprouts into a small plant and how it grows rapidly. They also learn about the natural life cycle of plants, about how to nurture living plants, and about where our food comes from! Even better, seedlings can provide plants for tending and brightening your class-

Watering is a favorite task.

room or for an outdoor garden. Be sure to keep a camera, notepad, and pencil handy to document the children's explorations.

If you begin with seeds, you can use commercially packaged seeds or seeds you've collected yourself from a previous harvest. You can also start plants from cuttings and bulbs to show all the different ways plants begin. Have fresh fruits and vegetables available during your engagements with planting and gardening. Cut them open and dissect them so the children can see, touch, taste, and smell each part of the fruits and vegetables. This will help the children really understand how fruits and vegetables come from plants that start from seeds.

When you're ready to begin, give the children seed-starter trays, terrariums, yogurt cups, fruit cups, or small planters. The children can use small scoopers, plastic spoons, or their hands to scoop soil into the containers. Give the children something tiny for holding the seeds so they don't drop the seeds while transferring them to the soil. (A lid or a tiny container works well.) Seeds all look different, so let children examine the seeds before planting them. Ask the children what they notice and how various seeds differ from one another. Make sure to label both seed containers and planted seeds with craft sticks or with masking tape and permanent marker. After the children plant their seeds, let them water their containers and place them in the sunlight.

Plant seeds in hanging shoe holders.

Planting seeds

Tip! Believe it or not, clear plastic over-the-door shoe holders are great for planting too! They offer multiple planting compartments and the ability to see the plant's development. Children can watch the seed open and sprout and watch the roots and stem develop. The plastic holds moisture inside, much like a terrarium. You can let the children spray the compartments with water bottles or water them with cups, watering cans, or eyedroppers. The shoe holder is portable, too! You can move it indoors and outdoors with ease.

It's easy to observe seeds' growth.

Tip! Place assorted seeds on individual index cards or small pieces of poster board or card stock. Label each type of seed and then cover the cards with contact paper.

GARDENING

For young children, there is no substitute for digging in the earth. Using their whole bodies to loosen the soil and dig in it is not only great fun, but is also terrific for good health! And it offers a wonderful opportunity to touch the dirt, smell it, and notice the worms and insects within it.

Plant whatever type of garden you have space for. It can be anything from a full-size garden to a window box. One simple idea is to fill a kiddie pool with soil. Voila—a portable miniature garden!

First, let the children prepare the soil by loosening it with trowels and hand rakes. Plant your garden from seeds or seedlings. Transplanting delicate seedlings offers children a wonderful opportunity to learn about gentleness and mindful care. It helps them understand what it takes to grow and harvest fruits and vegetables. Children love to water gardens! Give them plenty of buckets, watering cans, or a hose to have fun while engaged in this learning experience.

Readying the soil

Give the children the opportunity to see the harvest produced from their hard work. Harvesting is the joyful finale of their gardening experience. Let the children help pick the harvest, wash it, and eat it! Talk about healthy cooking and eating while you prepare and enjoy the fruits of your labors. And once again, be sure to take notes and photos throughout the process.

Planting and caring for young plants

. . . .

At one Montessori preschool in Minnesota, the children did a large-scale gardening project every year. The project began right after the winter break.

The children first planned their garden and chose the types of flowers, herbs, fruits, and vegetables they wanted to grow. They placed orders from seed catalogs and watched for the seeds' arrival in the mail.

Then, in the late winter or early spring, they planted and tended all the seeds indoors, in the classroom. They grew the seedlings in seed-starter trays placed on the shelves of large wheeled carts fitted with grow lights. They planted a lot of extra seeds—many more than their garden would accommodate.

When the time came for transplanting, they prepared the garden space outdoors and planted their garden. They sold all the extra seedlings to families and people in the community as a fundraiser.

As the various plants became ready for harvest, the children did the picking. They ate some of their harvest and donated the rest to people in the neighborhood.

. . . .

PROJECTS AND EXPERIMENTS

Listed below are a few projects and experiments that are enjoyable with younger children and offer opportunities to share the process of how seeds, bulbs, and plants grow. There are many variations to the projects described. Be sure to have your camera and pen and paper handy!

Seeds in a Baggie

All that is needed for this project is a simple ziplock bag, a few seeds, and some wet paper towels. There are a few variations to this experiment. Because the children always love spray water bottles, that is what I use.

First, write their names on the bags with permanent marker. Next, give them the bags, two green bean seeds, and one or two paper towels. Tell them to fold the paper towel and make a little bed, or "sleeping bag," for the seeds and tuck them in. Then tell them to lay the folded paper towel on a tray and let them spray all the water they want to on it. Have them carefully lift and tuck the dripping paper towel, with the beans laid inside, into the bag. Leave the bag unzipped a little to allow air space so the plant does not mildew. Then tape it to a window and watch the seed start to grow in a few days. Be sure to document and take photos along the way!

Carnations (or Daisies) with Colored Water

This experiment offers children the chance to really understand and visually see how a plant "drinks in" water and how water travels through the stem to make a flower change color.

Set out three or four containers or cups with water. Add different food coloring to each cup. Following a discussion about how plants "drink" water from the earth through their roots into their stems, ask the children what they expect to happen. Write down their answers. As the flowers begin to change color, you can discuss the reason for that and write down the children's thoughts and ideas.

Bulbs

Bulbs offer another opportunity to watch how flowers grow. Have two bulbs ready, one to plant and one that has begun its shoot to show the children the early growth. Plant the bulb in a container filled with soil or in the earth outside. Using containers, however, offers an excellent chance to chart and document growth within the classroom. And it is easy to "force grow" bulbs by putting them in a paper bag in the refrigerator or unheated basement for three months. When you take them out, the bulb will think it is spring!

Grass Heads

An easy craft project using sawdust and nylons (you'll find directions in appendix B), grass heads are fun for children to help create and care for. Glue the faces onto the nylons filled with sawdust. You can use wiggle eyes, pom-poms, and permanent markers to make the features. Tacky glue or thick craft glue works, although sometimes after several watering episodes pieces may loosen.

You can also do this project using a container filled with soil. In a paper cup or recycled container, simply add the soil and grass seed and watch the grass grow. Glue or draw the face directly on the container. The children can care for the grass heads, and as the grass grows, the children can use scissors to trim the grass "hair" over and over! They *love* this!

Tip: **Fill bins or a texture table with soil and grass seed. Add scissors and you'll provide an excellent opportunity to see how grass seeds grow—and to practice cutting!**

Observing Insects and Animals

There is no better way to learn about the natural world than through firsthand experience. Often this happens unexpectedly: we seize the moment, and the opportunity for learning unfolds. We give children a memorable lesson not only of facts but also of tenderness, compassion, and emotion for living things, as well as the impact we each have in the world. Likewise, in planning to collect or purchase insects or animals, children gain valuable information while being a part of the daily process of caring for them.

FROM CATERPILLARS TO BUTTERFLIES

A butterfly unit is a wonderful experience for even the youngest children. It is a magical look at the cycle of life in the most concrete way. Doing a full butterfly life cycle unit allows children to participate in the miracle of life this beautiful insect experiences.

It is wonderful to have the children involved in every step of the caterpillars' development. Show the caterpillars to the children on the opening day of the unit. (You can purchase live caterpillars from Insect Lore.) Children are naturally curious and seek to gain as much information as they can, and you may be surprised by the questions and discussions the children will engage in. Have ready a few of the many books available on the topic.

The rate at which the caterpillars grow is spectacular! Note all the changes the caterpillars go through. They will enter their pupa stage and remain there for a couple of weeks, depending on the species. While the caterpillars are in this stage, the children can help to get their new home (a net cage) ready for when they emerge from their chrysalises. They can gather a few flowers, a tiny container of water, and perhaps an orange slice. The materials can be switched every four days or so. Continue to watch, discuss, and journal the discoveries.

After the butterflies emerge, take them outdoors to set them free. Help each child get a butterfly on his finger, even if only for a second or two. Often the butterfly does not fly at all during the first few minutes, and if it does, it probably won't go too far right away. If necessary, try to lure the butterflies back onto your finger with a dandelion so you can give it to a child. It is very exciting to watch the faces of young children holding butterflies for the first time. The wonder that fills their eyes is incredible!

Try to obtain different species of caterpillars. Viewing the differences as the caterpillars metamorphose is very interesting. Whether you work with one species or several, be sure to document their development and take photographs along the way.

Observing . . .

A close-up look

Caterpillars grow rapidly.

The butterfly emerges.

Witnessing the wonder

Being gentle

FROM EGGS TO CHICKS

If you have the opportunity to offer children the amazing experience of watching the life cycle of a chicken, don't pass it up. It is a wonderful way to learn about the life cycle of a bird.

A great way to start an adventure like this is with the help of an experienced colleague or parent. If someone can loan you an incubator and some wisdom, you'll be well on your way to a successful project. Get eggs from a local farm and set them in the incubator. With the children, read books with pictures to discuss and understand what is happening inside the eggshell during the twenty-one-day incubation. Candle the eggs to see the chicks inside and observe them moving. This step brings the project to life in a very concrete way for the children.

The birth of the first chick will be a spectacular and unforgettable event! The children can witness the chick crack its egg and work itself out of the shell. Tired from its hard work, it lays its tiny head down on another egg. But within minutes, the little chick is up wandering around. The children will be amazed beyond words!

You can teach the children how to hold the chicks kindly and gently by using plush, battery-powered, chirping Easter chicks found at a discount store. Let the children be full participants in caring for the chicks, including feeding them.

A few notes of caution are needed. Children and adults *must* wash their hands immediately after handling the chicks or equipment used to care for the chicks. This unit must be done under adult supervision only. While the children are learning how to care for the chicks, be careful that they don't squeeze too hard or drop them, as the chicks can be squirmy!

Candling the egg

The first chick pecks the shell open.

An unfertilized, "eating" egg

Almost out!

Practicing holding soft chick

A young chick

First bites of food

Giving a gentle touch

FROM TADPOLES TO FROGS

Tadpoles to frogs is another great unit or project to embark on with children. Such incredible nature-filled science lessons provide the real-life learning in which children can take an active role.

Getting tadpoles from either the wild or a pet store offers children a chance to watch the life cycle firsthand. Set up the terrarium low enough for the children to see, and allow them to be full participants in the care of the growing tadpoles. Be prepared for it to be a bit of work on the adult's part. The terrarium may get a tad smelly, and sometimes the tadpoles do not survive and need to be scooped out.

If you collect tadpoles from the wild, be sure to add some of the water from the source where you collected them. Replenish this source water with each water change to keep them healthy. Also, be sure to release the frogs back into the wild when you are through caring for them.

Present the children with facts about the type of frogs you care for, and show them photos. This will help the children understand the frogs' needs.

Tadpoles

One day a group of children and their teacher found a praying mantis outside. They put it inside a cage, watched for a short period, and then released it. Finding out interesting facts about this creature and observing it was very intriguing for the children. The praying mantis was an insect the children had not seen before. But after an hour or so, it was time to let it go back into the natural world.

A praying mantis

A praying mantis close up

The teacher and the children took the praying mantis in a container to a grassy hill. They tipped the container on its side, but the praying mantis would not come out. They placed a stick in the container to make a bridge. But still the mantis would not move. The children and teachers waited and watched. This led to a lot of great conversation. Finally, around lunchtime, it began to rain. Together, the teacher and the children decided to leave the jar on its side where it was. They concluded that the praying mantis was safe inside the container and wanted to stay dry. They agreed to return the next day to see if it had left the jar.

When the group returned the next day, the praying mantis was no longer in the jar. Everyone took many guesses as to where it might have gone. Following this exciting experience, the children created a classroom book with all the photos and language the teacher had collected along the way.

HANDLING CRITTERS

Incorporate nature into your classroom on a daily basis by bringing the natural world indoors. Keep small containers and insect holders in a convenient place so you can quickly grab them as you head out. Be observant and seek out the unexpected critter encounter! Then, when you find caterpillars, frogs, worms, or insects, remember the following:

- Don't make uncomfortable faces when you touch insects and critters. Know which adults in the group are comfortable touching them, and let them be the ones who handle the critters.

- Know what creatures and insects in your region are safe to handle. Be certain you don't put yourself or the children at risk.

- Do research. If you don't know much about your newly found creature or insect, seek out information. Or do research in advance and then try to find a particular creature or insect in the natural world.

- Make sure you know what temporary living arrangement will be best for the creature or insect you find. We surely want to be respectful and cause no harm to any living thing, and we want to teach the children the same respectful message.

- Many children's books have wonderful photographs, stories, or facts to aid in your discovery. Keep them in your room for a while, either in the science area or book area.

- Children at this age often cannot be expected to hold creatures on their own. Even more experienced children will need an adult's hands right there, ready to assist or to take the creature back. Children have a tendency to pull their hands away quickly or even to squeeze too hard as they learn to care for small creatures. This very well may be a first experience for them in their young lives!

- During hot weather, be very mindful not to leave any creature or insect in the bright sun to bake in a container.

- Be sure to put the creature back into its natural world as close to where you found it as you can.

- Wash your hands and the children's hands immediately! Washing hands is imperative for this age group in particular, because many put their hands to their mouths so frequently. It is a good idea to carry moist wipes or baby wipes for a quick hand cleaning when you and the children are on walks.

A woolly bear caterpillar

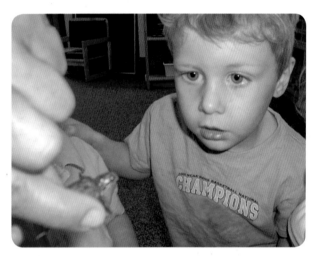

A turtle

A worm

Outdoor Exploration: Seeing What Nature Holds

Science investigations should take place not only indoors but also outdoors. Outdoor time offers children many benefits:

- breathing fresh air
- exercising their bodies
- developing a love of nature
- creating new experiences
- increasing knowledge of the world
- sharing experiences with adults and peers
- building cognitive, critical thinking, and problem-solving skills

Sharing nature with children helps them develop an appreciation of and attachment to the outdoor world. Children are naturally curious. They love exploring. They are not born with a fear of the natural world. They develop fear either from lack of experience or from observing fear in trusted adults—which is why it is so important for educators to take their role as nature guides seriously.

There is much to be learned in the natural world. The outdoors can become a second classroom if we allow it. Children need time to run freely, climb, and take risks, with adults encouraging the joy of free, uninterrupted play. Simply being still and noticing all that exists in the world around us is equally important. When we embrace every moment outdoors with excitement and make an effort to be in the moment *with* children, rather than simply supervising them, we share a lasting gift.

Explorations in the natural world can turn out to be the best moments in your program. Each time you go outdoors, you're sure to find something interesting that presents a teachable moment. Sometimes you may go out with a plan, but either the children or the environment leads you in another direction. Don't be afraid to stop and explore anything that presents itself. Whether it is a turtle, a cricket, a caterpillar, a grasshopper, a spider, or any other creature, plant, or object, you can collect it, examine it, take pictures of it, have a discussion about it, or look up facts about it in a book or on the Internet. You can make everything into a lesson. When you do so, children learn to become inquisitive and thoughtful about the world around them. They become true explorers.

. . . .

In my classroom, we consider nonliving items to be nature's treasures. If they're small enough, we collect them and bring them back to our science center to investigate. One time we found a long snakeskin. We took it back to school, photographed it, and put it in a clear plastic container to examine with a magnifying glass.

A snakeskin

. . . .

MY TREASURED POND

We all have different surroundings and environments to explore and incorporate into our curricula. You may need to explore your neighborhood without children first, to see what is available in your area. Areas that may appear a bit wild or un-traveled may be perfect natural areas to take young children when they are well supervised. Areas that are not maintained and that are not well known or frequently visited by people are wonderful homes for nature's creatures and plants. Such areas make fabulous outdoor classrooms! They offer numerous learning possibilities. Of course, we must take all necessary safety precautions when we take children to places offsite.

On the grounds where I work lies my treasured pond. I began going to the pond while working on my master's thesis. I designed, implemented, and documented an outdoor curriculum for my program. I also reflected on the effects of taking very young children to a wild area like the ones I played in when I was young. I was curious what the children would do, how they would interact, and how far I could comfortably involve them in nature. I found it amazing to watch the children develop a kinship with nature in this special place. And every year since, I have included my treasured pond in my curriculum. Over the years, I have found it equally fascinating to watch adults who are new to this environment!

My treasured pond

To get to the pond, we have to walk down the sidewalk, cross a bridge over a lovely small stream, cross the street, and enter a wide-open field with woods and a pond on the far side. On the first two visits, we hold hands for the whole walk. We talk a great deal about safety and following the rules to develop trust and respect. By the third visit, we let go of hands when we reach the field. What do you suppose the children do at that moment when they let go of hands and see a large open field stretching out in front of them? Of course, they run! It is a delightful sight!

The outdoor classroom

Full speed ahead!

The children know they are to stop at the opening of the woods. Adults are ready for anyone who may not understand or remember the first few times. Typically by this point, the children are interested, curious, and truly respectful of the rules—and they follow them. Once we enter the wild area of woods and pond, the children explore. Some pick up sticks, some run in circles, and others run straight toward the pond to see what's happening there. The children know where they must stop so they don't get too near the water. The pond is open,

and the children need constant supervision there. This area is where the true learning begins.

On each visit, the teachers give the children their nature bags. Each over-the-shoulder bag contains a pencil, a homemade clipboard, and a magnifying glass. The contents may change as the year progresses. The adults tell the children that they may collect nature's treasures if they can fit them in the bag. The rule is you cannot take anything that is alive or rip, pull, or detach anything that disturbs nature. Typically the treasures include rocks, fallen tree bark, sticks, feathers, interesting leaves, moss, and so on. Later we put the treasures in a clear bin for further investigation in our science area. We also use them at our texture table and for nature collage art.

Often I have a goal to guide what we do or look for during each visit. The goal can be as simple as noting seasonal changes or searching for animal tracks. Or it can be a more complex goal, such as reading a story about trees, insects, or wildlife and creating an activity around it. Sometimes our goal is simply to explore.

Deep exploration

Time for relaxing

Exploring

Reflecting

A firsthand experience

Time for pondering

Excitement!

I bring the digital camera, pens and pencils, small notepads, a backpack, and ziplock bags or containers for collections. I take photos of the children exploring, smiling, and pondering. I also photograph what the children see and note what they are saying or asking at that moment. Later I laminate many of those pictures and place them in the science center to be looked at with magnifying glasses. Or I make them into documentation panels explaining our discoveries and journeys.

Ready with a sketchpad

Outdoor painting

Since I began my journeys to the pond, I have noticed that these excursions help children develop a kinship with the natural world. They cultivate a true respect for living creatures and their environment, curiosity about the natural world, and a desire to explore and investigate. Children become more inquisitive, less fearful, more confident, more able to focus and reflect, and more knowledgeable. The children learn how to really see what is around them. They begin to hear the sounds of birds, insects, wind, and much else that escapes our ears every day. They learn to smell the scents in the air throughout the seasons. They become in tune with the natural world—and this takes practice. It is liberating, beautiful, and at times truly breathtaking to watch the learning and wonder in their little eyes.

LOG HOTEL

Start this activity by reading the picture book *Log Hotel* by Anne Schreiber. Discuss the story. Hand out bags containing magnifying glasses, pencils, notepads, and bug catchers. Walk to your favorite nature site. Search for a "log hotel." Look for any tree that has fallen and begun decaying. Look for the signs of decay shown in the book, such as rotting wood, insect life, holes, and so on. Speculate about what creatures may have lived and walked there. Share these questions:

- What do you think happened to the tree?
- What will happen to the tree?
- What does the tree feel like?
- What else do you notice?
- What should we do with it?
- What lived in this log?
- Do you think anything else may live in the tree now?

Take close-up photographs of the tree, of the children exploring the tree, and of any details the children or adults notice. Write down any language presented and received during this activity.

Search the area for trees that are more or less decayed. Note the differences. Photograph and discuss the differences. Later reflect on your experiences with the children. If possible, upload your pictures to a computer or print the photos to aid in classroom discussion.

Tip Let children touch and smell found objects. This helps them form a true understanding of their world, and it leaves an imprint in their minds forever!

Sticks at the pond

. . . .

The pond was my group's place for playing with sticks. The rules were these: no poking others and no running with sticks. Beyond that, if the child could lift it, then she could swing it! With the help of an adult, the child had to find a safe space to swing the stick, and then she had to let the others know she'd claimed the space for swinging. No one else was allowed in the space until the child with the stick was done swinging.

One very active boy in my group needed big body movement. He needed to explore his environment and his body within space. He was very sports motivated. One particular morning had been hard for him, and his behavior indicated he needed to get outside for some big movement in an open space. So we went to the pond, and the boy's body language and mood changed immediately.

He instantly went looking for a stick to use as a bat. He chose a few different ones and swung them a few times to try out the feel. I stayed with him, at a close distance, and reminded him to call out his safe swinging space to others. Eventually he settled on his "bat"—not simply a stick, but a tree branch five and a half feet long!

One adult who was new to our group walked toward us and almost entered the boy's swinging space. She shouted out that the stick was too big and told him to put it down. I politely reminded her and the child that this was the boy's safe swinging place, and that she and other children needed to step back out of the area until he was done. She walked away looking very unsettled.

The boy continued to swing, lift, drop, and retrieve the branch until he grew tired from it. The full-bodied movement, which must have been a liberating experience, left him feeling powerful, confident, and calm. Eventually he put the big branch back where he found it and left the swinging space to look for worms. And I took some time to connect with the unsettled adult to re-explain my philosophy. As with most things, one "rule" does not fit all, and it is my aim to tend to the individual needs of the children—even if it means swinging sticks!

. . . .

PLANNING FOR THE WEATHER

It is easy to step outside on a sunny, warm day. That feels good to everyone. But all too often, a cold, blustery, or rainy day discourages teachers and caregivers from taking their children outdoors.

Naturally the weather must have some effect on what we do outdoors and the length of time we stay outside. But only infrequently should it stop us from going outside all together.

How can we overcome our own personal weather distastes when it's too hot, too cold, too wet, or too whatever? How can we build a comfortable balance for the children in our care?

Many teachers struggle with this challenge. If you're one of them, reflect on your personal preferences and try to find ways to enhance outdoor experiences for yourself and your children.

For example, here are some strategies to use when it's hot or very sunny:

- Find shade.

- Have plenty of water for children and adults to drink.

- Take breaks from the heat or sun by resting in shady areas or going indoors briefly.

- Engage in water play with spray bottles, water tables, sprinklers, and so on.

- Take book baskets outdoors and place them under a tree or in some other shady spot.

- Take excursions to nearby shady places.

Here are some strategies to use when it's cold outside:

- Dress children warmly.

- Dress yourself warmly.

- Keep spare outdoor clothing available—especially mittens.

- Step inside to warm up often.

- Keep moving and keep busy!

Dressing for the weather

Soaking up the water

A good hat makes shade.

Snow gives the playground a new feel.

Digging deep in the sand

Getting close to the leaves

Sharing time outside

If it's raining, don't just stand by the window and watch. Get out in the rain as often as possible! Children *love* this experience. Playing freely in the rain and splashing in mud puddles are activities many children do not get to do often—if ever. They are used to hearing, "No! Don't jump in that puddle! Oh no! Look at your shoes; they're all muddy!" Once they figure out that you're not going to scold them for getting wet and muddy, they play in the rain with glee and gusto. It's great fun to watch.

Children love playing in the rain.

You *must* talk with families early on to explain that you believe it is important to get outside often—and that the children will often get messy. Let them know that you will go out every day, even in inclement weather. This is a great opportunity to let them know the importance of sending along spare clothes.

You may on occasion need to wash a particular outfit at school, but as a rule, it's okay to let the children go home a bit messy. Dirt happens. It is part and parcel of a day with little ones. Don't let worry about dirt interrupt meaningful moments and learning opportunities with children.

Encourage families to send their children in outerwear suited to each day's weather. For rainy days, promote rain jackets, ponchos, hats, boots, rain pants, and so on. Keep a supply of spares on hand too. Then you will always be prepared for a child who may be lacking on a particular day. Ask families—including past families—to donate outgrown outerwear for your box of spares. And be sure to carry lots of tissues when you play in the rain!

Enjoying the rain

Puddles!

Mud puddles are exhilarating!

Playing together in the rain

CHAPTER 6

Sensory Table

The sensory table is an important element in any classroom for two- and three-year-olds. Young children make sense of the world through their senses. A well-designed sensory table provides children with experiences that meet their need for exploring with their senses.

Benefits of Sensory Tables

What are the benefits of sensory tables?

- Sensory tables offer the opportunity to learn while using multiple senses (sight, touch, and smell).

- Sensory tables are soothing and calming.

- Sensory tables provide the sensory input twos and threes need for optimal growth and development.

- Sensory tables offer scientific exploration, conceptual learning, and cause-and-effect ex-

periences through pouring; measuring; sifting; scooping; mixing; distinguishing wet and dry, cold and warm, rough and smooth; and more.

- Sensory tables help children develop fine-motor skills through manipulating materials, pinching, pouring, sifting, grasping, and cutting.

- Sensory tables help children develop gross-motor skills (skills that use big muscles) through standing, stretching, reaching, passing, pouring, dumping, scooping, squeezing, stacking, and splashing.

- Sensory tables help children develop hand-eye coordination.

- Sensory tables help children develop social skills through peer interactions, sharing, give-and-take, compromising, and so on.

- Sensory tables help children develop their vocabulary and verbal communication skills as they share materials and space and make discoveries.

- Sensory tables help children develop independence, self-esteem, and creativity.

Planning Your Sensory Table

This chapter offers not only ideas for sensory materials to use at your table (sand, water, and so on) but also ideas for creating an exciting curriculum at the sensory table using specific themes or types of play. An effective sensory table offers both a variety of sensory experiences and a variety of ways to play. It offers both wet and dry materials and the opportunity to mix, pour, push, squash, and explore independently.

As you design your sensory table, consider providing a supply of small bins and trays. These give children a way to define their personal space at the table. Bins and trays create boundaries, letting children explore the sensory materials independently without other children invading their space. Different-colored bins and trays help very young children remember whose space is whose. And trays and bins with edges offer protection against spills. There are no guarantees, of course! For two- and three-year-olds, spilling is part of the fun.

You can set up your sensory table in any number of ways. However you do it, remember this: while adding more materials is certainly fun and appealing for children, offering ample time for exploration is equally important.

Plan carefully to minimize behavior problems at the sensory table. With a group of twos and threes, you may need to limit the number of children at the table. Too many children crowding one another can cause a great deal of stress and conflict. You may also find it helpful to increase the amount of materials or the number of items of the same sort within the table. For example, if driving toy cars through wet sand is a very popular activity, make sure you have plenty of cars and plenty of sand.

The sensory table is one area that is drastically different in a twos-and-threes room compared to a preschool room. For very young children, teachers must consider materials with great care, making certain that the table does not contain any items

that a young child might choke on. Avoid small pebbles, cedar chips, or similar items that could be hazardous if digested.

The sensory table should *always* be monitored! Young children need supervision to ensure that they do not put materials in their mouths, choke on small items, or get irritating substances such as salt, sand, or bubbles in their eyes.

Here are some general tips for planning your sensory table:

- All activities and materials should be open-ended, allowing the children to explore and develop ideas and critical-thinking skills.

- All activities should be fun, safe, and interesting.

- Regularly offer challenges and new experiences. These give children opportunities to explore, master new skills, build self-esteem and self-confidence, and form new ideas.

- Give children time for uninterrupted play. Children need time to explore, figure out, and manipulate materials freely.

- Always keep children's allergies a top concern.

- Be a guide and facilitator to children's learning and discoveries. Find a balance between standing back to let children explore and stepping in with questions (for example: "What do you think will happen as you add the water?").

Tip! Use ziplock bags to offer sensory materials to children with tactile sensitivities. Fill bags with fingerpaint or shaving cream and add sequins or glitter, if you like. Seal the bags shut, then tape the seals securely with masking tape to prevent leaks. Give the bags to children to manipulate, or tape them flat on the sensory table so children can rub their fingers and hands across the bags. Even though the sensory materials are sealed inside bags, supervision is still a good idea.

Suggested Materials and Play Items

The lists below include many sensory materials and play items that you could use in your sensory table or on individual sensory trays. Changing the materials and items will keep the sensory table interesting and challenging for the children in your program. Children benefit from both wet and dry materials. The lists offer some examples to begin with. You can add to them what best suits your program.

Sensory Materials	Play Items	
Sand	Scoopers (assorted sizes)	Playdough scissors
Soil	Nesting cups	Counting bears
Water (clear or tinted)	Containers and cups	Paintbrushes (assorted sizes depending on material)
Bubble water	Waterwheels	
Salt (plain or colored)	Sifters	Miniature pails
Glitter	Funnels	Boats
Snow	Sponges and scrubbers	Cars, trucks, and trains
Ice (Try adding salt!)	Small shovels	Rubber ducks or frogs
Shaving cream	Turkey basters	Artificial jewels
Pom-poms	Hand mixers	Plastic eggs (open-and-fill type)
Shredded paper	Nets	Rocks
Gak	Play dishes	Twigs, logs, and pine needles
Playdough	Pots and pans	Grass, hay, and leaves
Rocks	Baby dolls (various sizes)	Fabric flowers
Twigs	Toy animals (zoo, farm, and domestic)	Miniature boxes
Pine needles		Hair color brushes
Grass	Toy dinosaurs	Zen garden rakes
Hay	Toy sea animals	Small gutters
Leaves	Toy insects or snakes	Rubber tubes and small pipes
	Playdough cutters, tools, and rollers	Markers
		Tongs or tweezers

Mix and match the sensory materials and the play items however you like. Beginning here are a few ways in which you might offer the supplies suggested in the lists. These ideas work especially well in individual trays.

- playdough with golf tees and hammer, rocks, and jewels

- Gak with cutters and markers: The feel of drawing on gak's rubbery surface is quite different from drawing on paper. The marker color will eventually blend into the gak, changing its color.

- sand with animal figures or pots and pans and kitchen utensils

- snow with scoops

- salt with forest animals, plastic trees, rakes, and brooms

- soil with worker figures, shovels, and miniature wheelbarrows

- sand with vehicles, brooms, brushes, shells, or scoops

- shaving cream or goop with paint or with eye-droppers and liquid color

- twigs and pine needles with magnifying glasses

- water with funnels or waterwheels

- water with gutters and containers

The sensory table is both necessary and exciting for two- and three-year-olds. Sensory tables that work for your program will provide the children with many developmental benefits, as well as daily entertainment. Keep the area inviting through well-thought-out materials and aesthetically pleasing designs. Bring back favorites, and don't be afraid to try new and refreshing ideas!

Pressing gak through a basket

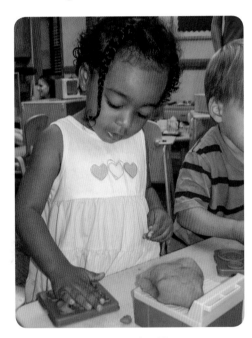

Playdough with toy ovens and molds

Playing with figures in a sensory tray

Gak with markers and scissors

Measuring cups work well—as do hands and fingers!

Pouring, pushing, and pulling the material

With snow, have gloves handy.

Salt with forest animals

Soil with construction figures

Shaving cream with paint

Sand and shells

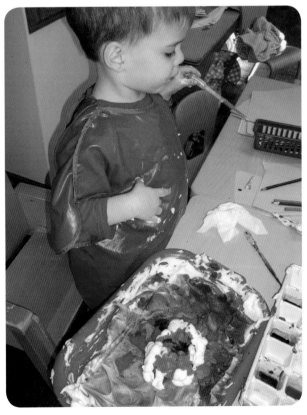

Shaving cream with liquid color and eyedroppers

Goop with liquid watercolors and eyedroppers

Fishing for treasure

Natural materials brought indoors

Pouring, pouring, and more pouring

Water fills and flows

A tray with soil, trucks, and figures

Tip! Keep a spare bin set aside for those tough moments or to quickly set up a one-person bin to provide the soothing sensory experience that gives a child some personal space away from the group.

An individual bin with sand and dinosaurs

An individual bin with blue water and ducks

An individual bin with soapy water, dishes, and sponges

CHAPTER 7

Circle Time

Circle time is an important portion of the day for two- and three-year-olds. It is a time to gather the group for fun, learning, discussion, and transitions. Circle time is where young children can learn to become members of a cohesive group, develop attention and focus, build cognitive skills, discuss concepts, share information, learn respect for others, practice taking turns, and develop social skills. Songs, fingerplays, and stories are often a big part of circle time. So are music and movement. Make sure you have adequate space to avoid bumps and accidents. Circle time is also an opportunity for presenting or modeling activities for the children.

What should circle time be for two- and three-year-olds? Here are some general guidelines:

- Circle time should be developmentally appropriate for two- and three-year-olds.

- Circle time should be brief—not longer than the children's attention span.

- Circle time should be respectful toward children.

- Circle time should be thoughtful and meaningful.

- Circle time should be relevant to children's lives, incorporating what they see and know.

- Circle time should be fun and exciting for children.

Many adults struggle to achieve balance among developmental appropriateness, fun, and learning in circle times. They may struggle to maintain children's interest, keep the gathering time short enough, create interactive and fun gatherings, establish boundaries, and be flexible. In addition, they may struggle to address issues with particular children while creating a fun and beneficial time for all the children. Rest assured, as teachers try different strategies and consult with others throughout, they will find solutions to make circle time the meaningful activity it can be.

Circle time activities should be planned to suit the specific needs and interests of your group; it's important to follow the children's interests. Sharing during circle time should include what the teacher wants to share, as well as what the children want to share. Teachers should continually revisit information at circle time, discussing what children have seen, done, or learned. Decide in advance if you want circle time to complement a theme in your curriculum.

As for all areas of the curriculum, circle time requires reflection. Throughout the year, step back and evaluate how things are going, what is working, and how you might change any aspects that aren't working.

Start Simple

In the beginning, circle time is the first opportunity you'll have to gather your children together as a group. As the year progresses, circle time is the place where the children will continue to unify as a community of learners. Get off to a good start by developing trust and respect, forming relationships, and integrating familiar ideas. A successful beginning will build a foundation for the year ahead.

During the first week or so of school, make it a goal to bring children over to circle time without forcing them. Offer fun and familiar activities to entice them into joining. Try starting with songs that most young children already know. This will give them a sense of security and comfort. For example, you might sing "Twinkle, Twinkle, Little Star" while handing out laminated stars the children can use to dramatize the song. Or you might sing a simple welcome song that incorporates the children's names. Other fun, familiar song choices are "If You're Happy and You Know It," or "Head, Shoulders, Knees, and Toes," or "The Wheels on the Bus."

Keep singing the same song at circle time for several days. This repetition will help the children know what to expect. Gradually and gently add new songs, short books, fingerplays, flannel board stories, or other interactive experiences.

Tip Be sure to take your circle time outdoors occasionally. Children adapt easily to the outdoor setting for circle time, and they enjoy the open space.

It is easy to create and use an outdoor gathering space. For seating, you can use logs, large rocks, large hollow blocks, or chairs. Almost anything you can do inside, you can do outside as well. In fact, sometimes outdoors is better! It provides more space and less worry about noise and mess.

An outdoor circle

Strategies for a Successful Circle Time

Often just beginning a song will send the message that you are ready to begin and will draw the children over to you. Younger children are "flockers." When one child moves, the other children often follow in groups.

As children arrive at circle time, offer laps for those who need them the most. Early in the year, allow children to hold comfort items such as blankets, small stuffed animals, small dolls, and so on if these are necessary or helpful.

Develop circle time routines early. Routines let children know what to expect and what they can rely on. But also be flexible. Have a plan, but keep it loose enough to allow letting go of it or moving in a different direction if necessary.

Get prepared ahead of time. Have all items you'll need ready on a shelf, tray, or elsewhere within reach so that when children are arriving at circle time, you are ready to receive them. If you are not prepared, they will quickly wander off and play elsewhere. Plan ahead for children who may have difficulty sitting with others. Arrange seating accordingly.

Be playful and warm and use humor to help children feel comfortable and engaged. Include the children's photos as props to help children recognize their own identities and others' identities and to promote the kinship of the group. If development among your children varies widely, you may want to consider having two separate circle times.

Keep the children involved and interested. Here are some tips:

- Don't make the circle time too long! Five minutes may be long enough in the beginning.

- Make sure the circle time encourages children to do something, not just listen.

- Design your circle times specifically for two- and three-year-olds, not preschoolers.

- Remember that props are highly successful with this age group.

- Use songs with movement to get children's attention quickly or help them refocus. Examples include "Jump Up (and Now Sit Back Down)," "Here We Go 'Round the Mulberry Bush," and "Open, Shut Them."

At the end of circle time, encourage the children to make choices and plans. As you mention or show the children available activities, they can decide where they want to go play. For example, you might ask, "What will your choice be?" or "Where will you start your play?" or "What are you thinking about first?"

The two- to three-year-old year is a good time for children to learn to keep their bodies in their own personal space and develop awareness of others' personal space. Children in this egocentric age group first need to understand what and where their space is. Next, they need to understand space expectations. Finally, they must learn to behave in ways that respect the space of others.

Define the sitting space for each child by using sit-upons. Having clear boundaries helps children stay in their own space, stay focused, and avoid distracting others.

Provide a consistent sitting space (sit-upon, chair, texture cushion) for children with special needs such as attention deficit disorder, sensory disorders, or autism spectrum disorders. Use laps if necessary, particularly at the beginning of the year, to help guide expectations. Help children with special needs keep focused by applying deep pressure to joints, using a soft shoulder touch, whispering in ears about important things that are happening, or offering a texture ball or Beanie Baby to squeeze or a chewing toy to mouth.

Here are several tips for keeping children sitting in their own space:

- Offer different-colored sit-upons. Sit-upons create boundaries. They say, "This is my circle; that is yours." They make clear the expectation of sitting in one's own space and not another's. They define the time for children: you are at the gathering circle with your peers. The task then becomes *keeping* the younger children at the circle.

- Fighting over colored sit-upons is a conflict sure to arise in some groups. The circular sit-upons common in many classrooms come in four colors, and teachers frequently face challenges in resolving squabbles over them. Often children have a favorite color and insist on it, and sometimes children on the spectrum *need* a certain color. One solution is to apply name tags to each sit-upon. Most teachers find that this simple move solves the problem. When it doesn't, try offering a choice between two available colors; tell a child she can just say, "No, thank you," to sitting on a circle that day; or let the child sit on a pillow instead. Remember, though: when you offer choices to one, you risk everyone wanting to be able to make choices, too, and it could get chaotic.

- Establish the rule that sit-upons are only for sitting on. If children play with the circles, they may bump into other children or become a distraction for people around them. In those cases, again, offer a choice: "You may sit on your circle or say, 'No, thank you,' and sit on the floor."

- You may be faced with children moving their circles to sit next to or *not* next to a particular child. And at times we *need* to make sure two children do not sit next to each other. Some successful strategies are writing children's names on strips of tape and attaching them to the floor to indicate who must sit where; offering a lap to a particular child; sitting next to the child who needs extra support so you

can provide a gentle touch, reminding him to attend to the circle; or having a particular child be a helper throughout the circle.

A gathering circle

Circle Time Web

Welcome
- Sing a familiar song
- Include photos!

Learning Activity
- Discussion with visuals
- Questions to ask with child participation

Songs
- Familiar
- With props
- Age appropriate
- With movement

CIRCLE TIME

Stories
- Books
- Puppets
- Flannel/felt sets
- Props
- Shadow show

What's Available
- Show/demonstrate
- Visual/display
- Encourage decision-making/ choices

Activity
- "What's missing?"
- "Feely box"
- "I have a riddle"
- Science experiment

This is a circle time web. It offers ideas of components that could be incorporated into a circle time. Not all the components would be used in one circle time. Instead, a teacher would choose components appropriate to the given day.

A Circle Time Example:

THEME: CATERPILLARS/BUTTERFLIES

Welcome Song	Learning Activity	Song	What's Available
"Little Red Box"	View live caterpillars in container. Discuss changes from last observation.	"I Wanna Be a Butterfly" (*Use props to show the stages of butterfly development.*)	Show tray with related activities available in the classroom centers.

This is an example of a circle time revolving around a caterpillar/butterfly unit. It incorporates a few components from the circle time web shown on page 114: a welcome song (any welcome song can be used); a learning activity related to the theme (aim to facilitate a rich discussion among the children); a second song, this one related to the theme (to hold children's interest, incorporate props to illustrate the lyrics, and use simple movements such as hand motions to keep children involved); and, last, a discussion of theme-related choice-time activities available in the classroom. This general circle time format could be used to support any theme.

Welcome Songs

Beginning a morning circle time with a welcome song helps you greet children and facilitates their transition into the school day. Using children's names and photos in the welcome song are personal and intimate ways to help them feel appreciated and included. Additionally, using names and photos helps children learn the names and faces of their peers. Consider keeping a sturdy set of laminated photos with the props for all your songs.

You will know what works with your group and what does not. Repetition is often best. Start with one song and repeat it for several days. You can then begin to weave new songs into your circle times. Try to strike a balance between familiar and novel. For children to feel comfortable enough to sing along, they need to feel they know the song and movements well. This takes a lot of practice and repetition for very young children. Repetition is particularly valuable when you have children with varying schedules who come only on certain days.

Children love the welcome songs listed below. This is just a small sample of the possibilities, though. Many early childhood websites offer more ideas. (See appendix C for more songs.)

GOOD MORNING SONG

Repeat this song as needed to sing all the children's names.

Good morning, Jacob!
Good morning, Paisley!
Good morning, Kia!
We're glad you came to school today.

LITTLE RED BOX

For this song, you might want to keep the children's laminated photos in a simple wooden box painted red.

> Oh, I wish I had a little red box
> To put my friend Brian in.
> I'd take him out and kiss, kiss, kiss
> And put him back again!
>
> Oh, I wish I had a little red box
> To put my friend Katrina in.
> I'd take her out and kiss, kiss, kiss
> And put her back again!

A photo peeks through the window.

Photos inside the "little red box"

I LOOKED THROUGH MY WINDOW

For this song, you can create a window prop with a picture frame. Take out the glass and hot-glue fabric onto the frame for curtains.

> I looked through my window,
> And who did I see?
> It's Jenny, it's Jenny
> Looking at me!

JOHNNY WHOOPS

Here are the finger movements for this song: Hold your right hand up with your palm facing you and your fingers spread. Hold your left hand up with only your pointer finger extended. Use your left pointer finger to touch each fingertip on your right hand one by one, starting with your little finger, moving toward your thumb, and then going back to your little finger again. Say "Johnny" (or the child's name) each time you touch a fingertip. Between the pointer finger and thumb of your right hand, slide your left pointer finger along your skin and say "whoops."

> Johnny, Johnny, Johnny, Johnny, whoops, Johnny!
> Whoops, Johnny, Johnny, Johnny, Johnny!

MARY WORE HER RED DRESS

Mary wore her red dress, red dress, red dress.
Mary wore her red dress—all day long!

HERE TODAY

Sing this song to the tune of "The Farmer in the Dell." Clap to the rhythm throughout the song.

Kara is here today, Kara is here today.
Let's all clap our hands and say, "Hip hip hooray!"

(Alternate version)
Tessa is here today, Tessa is here today.
Let's all clap our hands because Tessa is here today!

STAND UP

Sing this song to the tune of "Frère Jacques."

Stand up, Thomas. Stand up, Thomas.
Turn around. Touch the ground.
Reach up really high now.
Jump and touch the sky now.
Now sit down. Now sit down.

The "Stand Up" song outdoors

OTHER FAMILIAR SONGS

You and your children probably know most of the following songs, but you may not know all of them. (If you need lyrics for any of these, see appendix C.)

General Nursery Songs

- "Twinkle, Twinkle, Little Star"
- "Two Little Blackbirds"
- "Old MacDonald Had a Farm"
- "If You're Happy and You Know It"
- "Open, Shut Them"
- "Where Is Thumbkin?"
- "This Little Piggy"
- "The Itsy-Bitsy Spider"
- "I'm a Little Teapot"
- "Tommy Thumb"

Fall Songs

- "Make New Friends but Keep the Old"
- "The More We Get Together"
- "The Wheels on the Bus"
- "Who Are the People in Your Family?" ("Who Are the People in Your Neighborhood?")
- "Gray Squirrel"
- "Autumn Leaves Are Falling Down"
- "Way Up High in the Apple Tree"

Songs about Babies

- "Rock-a-Bye, Baby"
- "Good Night, Babies" (Tune: "Good Night, Ladies")
- "Kiss the Baby Good Night"
- "Hush-a-Bye, Baby"

Songs about Pets

- "Love, Love, Love Your Pets" (Tune: "Row, Row, Row Your Boat")
- "How Much Is That Doggie in the Window?"

Construction Songs

- "Drive, Drive, Drive the Truck" (Tune: "Row, Row, Row Your Boat")
- "I Wish I Were" (Tune: "If You're Happy and You Know It")
- "Do You Know What Tool This Is?" (Tune: "The Muffin Man")
- "This Is the Way We Use Our Tools" (Tune: "The Muffin Man")

Food Songs

- "On Top of Spaghetti"
- "Peanut Butter and Jelly"

Shopping Songs

- "A-Shopping We Will Go" ("A-Hunting We Will Go")
- "Let's Go to the Grocery Store" ("Mary Had a Little Lamb")

Bakery Songs

- "The Muffin Man"
- "Patty Cake"

Winter Songs

- "I've Got Two Warm Mittens" (Tune: "He's Got the Whole World in His Hands")
- "This Is the Way We Put on Our Mittens" (Tune: "The Muffin Man")
- "Five Little Snowflakes"
- "A Chubby Little Snowman"

Spring Songs

- "Rain Songs"
- "Rain, Rain, Go Away"
- "It's Raining, It's Pouring"
- "Springtime Rain" (Tune: "Twinkle, Twinkle, Little Star")
- "The Itsy-Bitsy Spider"
- "Five Little Ducks"

Butterfly Songs

- "I Wanna Be a Butterfly"
- "Caterpillar, Caterpillar"

Train Songs

- "Engine, Engine Number Nine"
- "Little Red Caboose"
- "Down by the Station"

Shape Songs

- "Do You Know What Shape This Is?" (Tune: "The Muffin Man")

Color Songs

- "If You're Wearing Red"
- "Do You Know What Color This Is?" (Tune: "The Muffin Man")

Songs about the Sun

- "You Are My Sunshine"
- "Mister Sun"

Frog Songs

- "I Want to Be a Frog Today"
- "Five Green and Speckled Frogs"

The Use of Props

Props encourage children to interact during circle times. Adding props to a simple or familiar song or story can change the experience dramatically for a very young child.

For example, when you sing the song "Five Little Ducks," use one large rubber duck and five small rubber ducks, along with a clear bin of water, as props. As the mother duck says, "Quack, quack, quack," in the song, place one duck in the water, and so on.

Similarly, when you sing the song "Five Green and Speckled Frogs," you could use five green rubber frogs, a small log or piece of bark, and a bin of water. As each frog jumps into the pool during the song, you place a frog in the water.

Five green and speckled frogs!

After using props for circle time, place the props at the sensory table. Children will enjoy an encore of the songs or stories while playing with the materials!

Literacy Activities

Circle time is a great opportunity for literacy activities. Children love books and other means of storytelling. While children are gathered together in a circle, you can introduce stories and authors, share meaningful books, and open the door to literacy for very young children.

A twos-and-threes classroom often is not the appropriate place to teach children their ABCs. But it *is* where literacy begins. Very young children acquire literacy through looking at books and hearing stories read aloud, through classroom activities that develop language, and through seeing words in print—not through direct instruction and practice. If you use themes in your curriculum, circle time is perfect for using the theme to develop literacy.

It is important to choose storybooks appropriate for this age group and for your particular group. Begin circle time literacy units about midyear. (See "Thinking about the Whole Year" on pages 6–7 for more on this topic.) You might start with these storybook favorites:

- *The Mitten* by Jan Brett

- "Goldilocks and the Three Bears"

- "The Three Little Pigs"

- *Owl Babies* by Martin Waddell

- *Gingerbread Baby* by Jan Brett

- Nursery rhymes

- Picture books by Eric Carle, such as *Brown Bear, Brown Bear, What Do You See?*, *The Very Hungry Caterpillar*, *The Very Busy Spider*, or *Papa, Please Get the Moon for Me.*

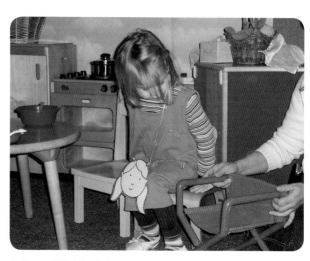

Acting out "Goldilocks"

Acting out Owl Babies

Acting out "Little Miss Muffet"

EXTENDING LITERACY: ERIC CARLE

Eric Carle's large collection of picture books is a favorite among this age group. In my classroom, we squeeze every bit of learning, fun, and beauty we can out of Carle's books. We do an Eric Carle unit that lasts anywhere from two to four weeks, depending on the interest of the group. It delves deeply into both literacy and art.

We read one Carle book each day during our Eric Carle unit. I begin with simple and familiar ones, such as *Brown Bear, Brown Bear, What Do You See?* or *The Very Hungry Caterpillar,* and then move on to more complex books, such as *The Very Quiet Cricket* or *Today Is Monday.* Meanwhile, I dole out bits and pieces of information about Eric Carle

himself gleaned from the Eric Carle Museum of Picture Book Art in Amherst, Massachusetts, the video *Eric Carle: Picture Writer,* and the book *The Art of Eric Carle.*

I then show the children how to make authentic "Eric Carle papers" and use those papers to create collage pictures. Through this component of the Eric Carle unit, children learn that they, too, can be authors and illustrators using their own words and creativity. This section explains the steps I use to show children how to create art similar to Eric Carle's. (When I refer to "Eric Carle papers," this means the individual painted papers that serve as collage materials.)

Eric Carle creates his illustrations through collage. First, Carle paints on tissue paper. He paints many designs in assorted colors and then cuts the tissue paper to create the illustrations. What I do differently is wrap the tissue paper around poster board or cardboard before the children paint on it to keep it from ripping. After the painted tissue paper is dry, I carefully untape it from the cardboard, which I reuse for the next round of tissue paper painting. The painted tissue paper is quite delicate. I teach the children to treat the paper gently, and they soon begin to use the same language. Here is the process I follow:

Each day, I choose two or three colors of paint. I also select shades and tints of these colors. I wrap white tissue paper around the cardboard or poster board. And then we paint several using assorted brushes or rollers.

Over the next several days, I teach different techniques used by Eric Carle, such as splatter-painting, drawing the handle of the paintbrush across the wet painted tissue paper, or painting with small carpet or burlap scraps (I cut small pieces of remnant carpet or burlap, as Carle would, and dip them into the paint to make a novel print). To support the children's understanding, I show the children illustrations in Carle's books made using these techniques. In a large box, I collect the painted "Eric Carle" papers until we have enough, which usually takes about seven or eight days. Each child gets to paint her own papers, but I do not mark them with names or keep them separated from the group's. All of the painted tissue paper simply gets put in the box. The children can make as many as they want.

Then we begin the cutting process. I gather all the painted tissue paper from the box, and the children begin to cut it into little pieces. I also offer the children oil pastels to use for drawing on the painted papers, adding a second layered element as Eric Carle does.

The next step is offering glue sticks or glue with brushes. The children now begin the collage and laying process. We use simple construction paper for them to glue their pieces to. They are encouraged to design their work any way they please.

Several days or weeks into the Eric Carle unit, I read special stories, such as *Mister Seahorse.* I love that book! In it the daddy seahorse carries the eggs in his pouch. He travels the ocean, greeting other daddies also tending to their eggs. In the end, the daddy's eggs hatch, and one baby tries to get back in the pouch. In a bittersweet moment, the daddy seahorse tells the little seahorse he must head off into the ocean. This story, like many of Eric Carle's, has a message within. It's delightful to see the children's dear faces during such stories. Another exciting part about *Mister Seahorse* is its special pages; the fish are hidden or camouflaged behind layers of sea rocks, coral, and seaweed that are printed on layers of translucent plastic pages. I try to simulate this technique using clear sheet protectors cut in two, which works perfectly! I put out permanent markers and small amounts of acrylic paint for the children to use to draw and paint on their clear sheets. Then they place their clear sheets on top of their tissue paper collage. The effect matches that achieved in the pages of *Mister Seahorse*, and the children are amazed! Because I don't typically use permanent markers and acrylic paint in my room, I am right there with the children to be certain the materials are used carefully. As always, safety measures need to be followed.

Next, we read stories such as *The Secret Birthday Message* and *Watch Out! A Giant!* Both of these books have fun die cuts and other surprises on each page. The children love to ponder *Watch Out! A Giant!* because it's a story that stirs their emotions. In it, the reader is led to believe the story is about a scary giant; the die cuts and flaps surely encourage you to think it is. But in the end, the reader learns that the children in the story are just playing a make-believe game *about* a scary giant. *Watch Out! A Giant!* can start a wonderful discussion about the difference between real and make believe.

After we finish reading, we return to our collages to simulate the die cuts in these Eric Carle books in our own work. We use scissors and large circle hole punches to cut doors and windows. While they work, the children dictate their own stories. Sometimes they dictate an original story, and sometimes they dictate a favorite Eric Carle story. The teachers write down the children's stories and attach them to their artwork. And once they have finished creating their Eric Carle pages and Eric Carle–inspired books, the unit is complete! The photos that follow show the process of the Eric Carle paper techniques. Even two- and three year-olds can successfully produce this amazingly authentic Eric Carle–style artwork!

Painting our own Eric Carle papers

One large Eric Carle tissue and poster board project

Using tissue paper over poster board

Using a carpet scrap to paint

Cutting the painted tissue paper

Both glue sticks and brush-on glue work well.

Using oil pastels

Beginning the layering process

Gross-Motor Activities: Music and Movement

Young children need lots of exercise. That's why it's essential to plan your program with a healthy balance of indoor and outdoor movement. If your program relies on indoor space for gross-motor activities, finding new ways for children to move their bodies may be a challenge. Space may also be an issue. You'll have to be very creative and mindful to make sure you plan enough opportunities.

Music and movement activities at circle time are a fun and appropriate way for two- and three-year-olds to meet their gross-motor needs. They love to move their bodies, dance and twirl, play musical instruments, play games, and challenge themselves physically. When you offer music and movement at circle time, you are helping children gain many important skills and benefits, such as listening, following directions, exercising, following rhythm and melody, and having new experiences.

With twos and threes, it's a good idea to be prepared for both planned movement activities and unplanned movement needs. Planning is important for the timing of gross-motor activities. You need to balance high-energy and low-energy activities throughout your day. For example, you would not want to plan a high-energy activity right before rest time.

Sometimes children unexpectedly need to move their bodies. To meet this need, you can have movement activities and supplies ready to go. It is best to be prepared for unexpected movement needs so you can meet them before they turn into rambunctious play. Try to have specific activities in mind to meet the specific needs of individual children. Make use of any space you can find—and temporarily take over. For example, use the hallway, unoccupied rooms, stairs, and the outdoors! Children of this age group love spontaneous playful moments with their caregivers and peers.

Following are many music and movement activities and materials you can incorporate into your program.

MUSIC

Music CDs are a pleasant and useful addition to circle times with young children. Some favorite artists for twos and threes are Greg and Steve, Raffi, Hap Palmer, Barb Tilsen, Putumayo Kids, Dan Zanes, and Wee Sing.

Scarf dancing

MUSICAL INSTRUMENTS

Musical instruments are valuable materials in early childhood classrooms. They provide children with the opportunity to add and create music, as well as learn about a variety of instruments. Using musical instruments is useful in circle time, as well as at specific music and movement times during which children have the opportunity to move and challenge their bodies. Examples might include a parade, jumping and bending, or following movement instructions with musical instruments.

SONG AND GAME IDEAS

- "Head, Shoulders, Knees, and Toes": While singing the song, have the children follow your movements of tapping each body part. Younger children love doing it faster a second time.

- "Hokey Pokey": Have children put into the circle the appropriate body part to "shake" when prompted, and allow them to dance the "hokey pokey" when directed in the song, turn, and give a clap.

- Freeze Dance: The freeze dance can be done with any music, although there are music CDs with specific pauses for freeze movements. Allow the children to dance freely. When the music stops, they freeze.

- "Ring around the Rosie": While singing the traditional nursery rhyme song, have the children hold hands, turn in a circle, and gently fall to the ground when prompted.

- What Time Is It, Mr. Bear?: This game is played outside or in a large open space. The children all line up against a fence or wall. The teacher and a child or two will be Mr. Bear and stand facing away from the other children, far enough away from them to be able to run (about twelve paces). The children (and perhaps another adult at first, until the children learn how to play the game) yell, "What time is it, Mr. Bear?" Mr. Bear answers, "One o'clock," and the children all take one step toward Mr. Bear. The children will yell again, "What time is it, "Mr. Bear?" Mr. Bear answers the time, and they take the same number of steps toward Mr. Bear. Continue until all the children are close to Mr. Bear. Mr. Bear will answer, "It's *midnight*!" Mr. Bear then chases the children back to their starting place. The first person Mr. Bear touches will be the new Mr. Bear. While learning to play and follow directions, the teacher can just choose who will be next.

- Red Light, Green Light: In a gentler version of this game, it is not a win or lose game. The teacher usually would be the person to play the "stoplight," and the children try to touch her. To begin the game, all the children line up against a fence or wall, a good distance from the stoplight (teacher). The teacher faces away from the line of children and shouts, "Green light." The children (and perhaps another adult until the children understand the game) move toward the stoplight. At any point, the stoplight can shout, "Red light!" and turn around. If any of the children are caught moving, they go back to the starting space. Often with the younger ages you don't fuss over making them stop while they're learning how to follow the directions of the game. The game resumes again as the stoplight turns back around and shouts, "Green light!" The first child to touch the teacher can either be the stoplight or join the teacher in being the new stoplight. The fun is really more playing and following directions for this age group, not the winning and losing. A good place to introduce the "red light, green light" concept is on a bike path.

- Duck, Duck, Goose: Use the simple and gentle version.

- "Bazooka-Zooka Bubblegum": "Sticky, Sticky Bubblegum" follows this song nicely.

> My mom gave me a penny
> To go and see Jack Benny.
> But I didn't see Jack Benny.
> Instead, I bought bubblegum!
> Bazooka-zooka, bubblegum,
> Bazooka-zooka, bubblegum.
>
> My mom gave me a nickel
> To go and buy a pickle.
> But I didn't buy a pickle.
> Instead, I bought bubblegum!
> Bazooka-zooka, bubblegum,
> Bazooka-zooka, bubblegum.
>
> My mom gave me a dime
> To go and buy a lime.
> But I didn't buy a lime.
> Instead, I bought bubblegum!
> Bazooka-zooka, bubblegum,
> Bazooka-zooka, bubblegum.

My mom gave me a quarter
To go and buy some water,
But I didn't buy water.
Instead, I bought bubblegum!
Bazooka-zooka, bubblegum,
Bazooka-zooka, bubblegum.

- "Sticky, Sticky Bubblegum": This song perfectly follows "Bazooka-Zooka Bubblegum."

  (Spread your fingers and wipe them together back and forth as you sing the first three lines. Pretend your hands are covered with bubblegum.)

  Sticky, sticky, sticky bubblegum,
  Sticky, sticky, sticky bubblegum,
  Makes my hands stick to my... knees! *(Stick hands to knees.)*
  So I pull, and I pull... and I pull...
  Until I'm... free!

  Sticky, sticky, sticky bubblegum,
  Sticky, sticky, sticky bubblegum,
  Makes my hands stick to my... nose!
  So I pull, and I pull... and I pull...
  Until I'm free!

  (Repeat with different body parts, and "pull them free." Give each child a chance to decide where their hands are stuck.)

- "If You're Happy and You Know It": Follow the song with appropriate actions.

  If you're happy and you know it, clap your hands! *(clap, clap)*
  If you're happy and you know it, clap your hands! *(clap, clap)*
  If you're happy and you know it, and you really want to show it.
  If you're happy and you know it, clap your hands! *(clap, clap)*

  (Alternate verses)
  If you're happy... shout, "Hooray!"
  If you're angry... stomp your feet! *(stomp, stomp)*
  If you're sad... cry, "Boo hoo!"

  If you're sleepy... give a yawn, "Ho hum."
  If you're friendly... wave, "Hello!" *(wave arm)*
  (You could also do three actions and end with the following line.)
  If you're happy and you know it do all three! *(Clap, clap! Stomp, stomp! "Hooray!")*

- "Tooty-Ta": There are several versions of this song. It is an echo song. Children and adults form a circle and sing the chorus and add in each additional action and movement. Each chorus is sung while turning in a circle.

  CHORUS: A tooty-ta, a tooty-ta, a tooty ta-ta!
  A tooty-ta, a tooty-ta, a tooty ta-ta!
  Thumbs up *(chorus)*
  Thumbs up, elbows back *(chorus)*
  Thumbs up, elbows back, knees together *(chorus)*
  Thumbs up, elbows back, knees together, feet apart *(chorus)*
  Thumbs up, elbows back, knees together, feet apart, bottoms up *(chorus)*
  Thumbs up, elbows back, knees together, feet apart, bottoms up, head back *(chorus)*
  Thumbs up, elbows back, knees together, feet apart, bottoms up, head back, tongue out *(chorus)*

- "Jump, Jim Joe": Hold hands with a partner and follow actions.

  Jump, jump, jump, Jim Joe!
  Nod your head and shake your head and tap your toe.
  'Round and 'round and 'round you'll go.
  Then you find another partner and
  You jump, Jim Joe!

  (Jump with children while holding hands with partners. Nod, shake, and tap. Next, turn and spin and sing until "find another partner." Children drop hands and find their

next partners' hands, and repeat the song and dance.)

- "Jump (and Now Sit Back Down)": Allow one child at a time to stand and jump while singing the following song: "Suzy, Suzy, jump up and down, jump up and down. Suzy, Suzy, jump up and down. Then . . . sit . . . back . . . down."

- "The Wheels on the Bus": Follow all hand motions while singing the song (extend and roll arms for the wheels going round and round, and continue for each action in the song).

- Simon Says: Don't worry about doing the "I didn't say, 'Simon Says,'" portion with younger children. Simply have children follow your steps and commands to this game or other "follow me" games.

- "Punchinello": To begin, have the children form a circle with one child in the center as "Punchinello." Punchinello does an action (such as hop up and down, spin around, and so on) while the children sing the song.

    What can you do, Punchinello, funny fellow?
    What can you do, Punchinello, funny you?

    (The children, still in a circle, copy the action that Punchinello is doing, and sing the following.)

    We can do it, too, Punchinello, funny fellow.
    We can do it, too, Punchinello, funny you!
    You choose one of us, Punchinello, funny fellow,
    You choose one of us, Punchinello, funny you!

    (Punchinello selects another child as Punchinello and takes the child's place in the circle. The song continues until every child who would like a turn gets one.)

- "Skinnamarink"

    CHORUS:
    Skinnamarinky dinky dink, *(Put one hand under the opposite-arm elbow and wiggle hand of the stretched-out arm like an elephant.)*
    Skinnamarinky doo, *(Switch arms and repeat motion.)*
    I love you! *("I"—point to self. "Love"—fold arms across chest. "You!"—point to child.)*
    (Repeat chorus.)
    I love you in the morning *(Make a circle by holding your hands; then keep arms down and lightly swing them back and forth.)*
    And in the afternoon. *(Same motion as above, but move arms up to chest level.)*
    I love you in the evening *(Same motion as above, and move arms up over head.)*
    Underneath the moon. *(Make a circular motion around body with arms.)*
    (Sing chorus once more.)

- "Teddy Bear, Teddy Bear"

    Teddy bear, teddy bear, turn around. *(Turn around in circle.)*
    Teddy bear, teddy bear, touch the ground. *(Touch the ground.)*
    Teddy bear, teddy bear, show your shoe. *(Point one foot out.)*
    Teddy bear, teddy bear, that will do. *(Wave a finger.)*
    Teddy bear, Teddy bear, run upstairs. *(Run in place, or motion to go upstairs.)*
    Teddy bear, Teddy bear, say your prayers. *(Put hands together.)*
    Teddy bear, Teddy bear, turn out the light. *(Pretend to turn out light.)*
    Teddy bear, Teddy bear, say good night. *(Fold hands under head and pretend to sleep.)*

BEANBAG SONGS AND GAMES

Young children enjoy beanbag songs and games. Beanbags are often sold in packs of various colors and sizes. There are several CDs with music and directions for playing the games. These games offer good opportunities for moving large muscles, developing good hand-eye coordination, following directions, working together, staying on task, and building other skills. My favorite CD for years has been *Bean Bag Activities and Coordination Skills* by Georgiana Stewart.

PARACHUTE GAMES AND SONGS

Children love using the parachute. It is an activity that inspires a lot of giggles and excitement. Parachute play is a good activity on days when going outdoors is not possible—although using a parachute outdoors is great too! Parachutes come in a variety of sizes. For the younger ages and smaller groups, little parachutes with eight or ten handles are perfect. Younger children enjoy the songs and games that can be sung and played while using the parachute. What follows here is just a very small sampling of the many songs and games that are available. (Lyrics can be found in appendix C.)

Parachute play

- "We're Going to Kentucky": Children sit on the floor holding the parachute's handles. One child sits on the hole in the center, and the other children lift the parachute sides up and down. The child is asked whether he would like the song sung fast or slow. The faster it is sung, the bigger the movement from the parachute for the child.

- "Where, Oh Where Have the Children Gone?": Children sit on the floor bunched together while the teachers stand holding the parachute over the children's heads. The parachute is lifted up and down with more force to make it full above. The song is sung, with the final verse ("There . . . they . . . are!") sung slowly. Then the teachers shout, "Run!" And the children run and then come back to repeat. They never seem to tire of this!

- "This is the Way . . ." : Various tasks can be repeated for this song, such as "This is the way we skip all around," "jump all around," "turn to the right (left)," "hop up and down."

- "Old MacDonald Had a Farm": While holding the parachute handles and waving the parachute up and down, the children toss soft farm animals one by one into the parachute to make them raise up and down.

- "Ring around the Rosie": Children hold the handles of the parachute and wave it up and down while turning in a circle.

OTHER WAYS TO ADD MOVEMENT TO YOUR DAY

Following are many ideas for adding gross-motor movement into your day. Some activities can be planned in advance, and some can be used on a moment's notice during a high-energy situation! In such a situation, the key is to take control so the activity flows smoothly. Here are some games and items that will get children moving:

- an obstacle course to climb inside, over, and around; balance on; and so on

- scooters, small ride-on cars, and other riding toys for use in a large, open room or a hallway, if possible

- shopping carts or baby strollers to go up and down halls or other open space

- Nerf indoor basketball hoops that can be easily set up and moved as needed

- indoor-safe ball, using plastic Easter eggs for balls and empty paper towel tubes for bats (baseball, soccer, kickball)

- volleyball using beach balls and a temporary net (When children are over three, you can consider using balloons for a light and safe "ball-like" item. Temporary nets can be as simple as bright-colored yarn tied across the room. The bright color makes it easy to see so no one runs into it.)

- yoga

Yoga benefits even the youngest of children.

- hopping games (into circles, squares, or over tape)

- hula hoops (jumping or stepping through them while holding them up or laying them on the floor)

- bikes in a large open space (Make masking tape "bike tracks" to keep children in bounds.)

- bikes lifted onto a large hollow block to make them stationary (Children will get to pedal, but the bike won't move.)

- "Row, Row, Row Your Boat" song and movements (with a partner holding hands)

- Follow the Leader game

- simple ball toss and catch

- hopscotch (simple version)

- marching and parade games

- "We're Going on a Bear Hunt" song and movements (with objects to climb over and through)

- jumping games

- exercises (jumping jacks, stretches, side twists)

- exercise mats (rolling, crawling, hopping)

- frog hop, bunny hop, duck walk, snake crawl, fish swim, and other animal movements

- balance beam (easily made with long wooden unit blocks, boards, and tape)

- bubble catch (not on slick floors)

- activities with nursery rhymes ("Jack Be Nimble," "Jack and Jill")

- tape on floor for children to step in, jump over, stop at

- games that encourage keeping a rhythm or beat; going fast and slow; moving up and down; singing high and low

- dance parties

CHAPTER 8

Dramatic Play

Dramatic play is a popular curriculum area for twos and threes. Through dramatic play, children develop and enhance their social skills. Children often begin dramatic play in parallel mode, playing near—not with—one another. But soon they begin more skillful and cooperative play with their peers.

Throughout the year, dramatic play increases in complexity and expands in variety. Children learn to share materials, negotiate with one another, take turns, be patient, and cooperate. They learn how to use their imaginations and assume the perspectives of different characters. This helps them develop empathy toward others. Children also often develop math and literacy skills through dramatic play. For example, while playing restaurant, children might use cookbooks, recipe cards, cash registers, pretend money, books about food, and so on as props.

Start Simple

Start your dramatic play center very simply. Consider setting it up as a home or family scene first. This setting will be familiar and comforting to chil-

dren at the beginning of the year. Include general housekeeping items, items to tote around, baby dolls, and soft animals.

Keep the dramatic play area the same for several weeks while the children get to know the environment, build routines, and establish relationships with you and their peers. Keeping things simple and predictable also allows you time to observe the children. During these first weeks, you become familiar with each child and the group dynamics.

Keep items simple and familiar.

Following are some popular items with which to start your dramatic play area. You can gradually add more as the year goes on.

- baby dolls with a few clothes and blankets, a baby bed, and a high chair

- basket or bin full of purses and small tote bags

- basket of play telephones and sets of toy keys

- play food and play dishes—but not an overwhelming amount

Changing the Dramatic Play Environment

After four to six weeks, start adding some dramatic play props that dovetail with your curriculum themes. As your themes change, switch out props and change the setting.

Changing the setting will change how the children play in the dramatic play center. It might change who comes to play there too. A new setting provides different role-playing opportunities and new experiences within the familiar environment of your classroom.

Following are some theme ideas for your dramatic play area. These are just a few examples. No doubt you will come up with many more! By observing the children's dramatic play, you can plan new settings and props tailored to the interests and needs of your group.

- home and family life

- baby nursery

- pet shop

- veterinary clinic

- seasons (winter scene, spring scene, summer scene, and fall scene)

- nature setting with wildlife components such as frogs and butterflies

- beach

- construction site

- restaurant

- grocery store

- bakery

- train station

- greenhouse or florist shop

- fairy tale or castle (with an emphasis on literacy, castle building, and royal role play, not swords and dragons, which might be scary or develop into unsafe play)

The restaurant-themed dramatic play area

Playing restaurant

The construction workshop

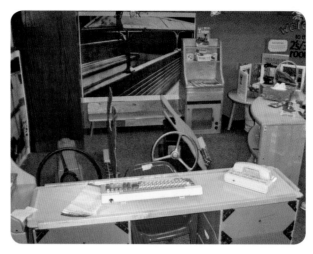

The train station

Working hard at a desk

The nature and butterflies dramatic play area

Driving the train

A castles and fairy tales theme area

Playing bakery

The Owl Babies *nest*

Gender in Dramatic Play

Dramatic play should avoid assigning children to gender roles and instead accommodate roles that both boys and girls will feel comfortable assuming. More neutral props and costumes serve a double purpose. They let children choose their own roles without forcing or leading the choices. And they make all children feel welcome in the dramatic play area.

In the past, many boys felt pressure from adults *not* to dress up in costumes or play with dolls. That pressure has abated, but it still exists. To counter it, make sure that boys feel welcome to play just as freely as girls do in your dramatic play center.

Young children generally have the attitude that dresses are for girls. Our culture promotes this idea too. By minimizing superfancy props such as dresses, jewelry, and sparkly shoes, you can make your dramatic play area inviting to girls and boys alike. You might also consider the fact that fancy props promote superficial language, such as the words *pretty* and *beautiful.* You can encourage children to use more meaningful vocabulary by providing props that support it.

Open-ended dramatic play materials encourage children to be creative and imaginative without forcing them into roles. For example, children can use large scarves to become whatever characters they wish. Boys wrap up in scarves as enthusiastically as girls do. Search your local dollar store for big, long, silky, and colorful scarves. Or buy some inexpensive material from a fabric store and use it to make flat panels of fabric with Velcro straps for fastening. A few other open-ended materials that both boys and girls can enjoy are small bags (not just purses), old cell phones, cameras, and hats.

Scarves make a good open-ended material

Managing Your Dramatic Play Area

Following are some tips for managing your dramatic play center:

- Make your dramatic play center as spacious as possible.

- Keep the area tidy and free of clutter.

- Make the area aesthetically pleasing.

- Begin with a basic and predictable setting.

- Keep items in baskets or clear bins where children can grab them easily—and you can clean them easily.

- Encourage the children to participate in cleaning.

- Be careful not to provide items that are choking hazards.

- Have a bin nearby for depositing mouthed items for cleaning.

- Children at this age love to collect and tote things! Have plenty of items to collect, as well as small baskets with handles for toting.

- Provide duplicates (at least two or three) of popular props.

- Carry over some props from one unit to the next if children are very interested in them.

- Know your children and remember that each group is different.

- Observe and record how children use the area and how well they seem to like it. Take pictures!

Tip! Every now and then, put away items for a few weeks or months; then return the items so children can enjoy them again. Their renewed excitement is fun to watch!

Here are some common items you might use in your dramatic play center throughout the year:

- bags, baskets, and small duffel bags

- keys, wallets, old credit cards, pretend money, and old cell phones

- computer keyboards, telephones, and cameras

- baby dolls, doll clothes, baby blankets, and bottles (if no children still use bottles)

- doll high chairs and doll beds

- play food, play dishes, and tea sets

- stuffed animals and Beanie Babies

- tool kits and doctor kits

- small books

- silky scarves

- small pillows

- old calendars and date books

- clipboards with paper and pencils

- unbreakable mirrors

- flowers and vases

- doilies

- child-made props.

Caring for the babies

Your Role

There is a fine line between being a facilitator for young children and being a playmate. It is important to be the former, not the latter.

Adult facilitation is pivotal for very young children in the beginning of dramatic play. With this age group, adults need to set the stage. We need to model what happens in a particular setting. For example, we need to show children that a pet shop needs a customer looking for a new pet and supplies, as well as a store worker to sell items and care for the animals. In a construction setting, we might show children that the worker has a workbench for building, and the foreman has a desk with plans, a phone, and a camera to inspect jobs or to arrange new ones.

After we model for children and set the stage for play, children quickly follow our lead and begin to play in a similar way. Soon the children are involved enough for us to pull back, let them develop their own ideas, and interact independently. Our goal is for children to play with one another rather than rely on us to lead the dialogue and action. If we drive the play, the children will not know how to play without us. To develop independent and creative thinkers, we need to give children ample time and space in which to form their own ideas and try them on one another.

It is important to be available, of course—particularly early on. But try to scaffold only as much as is necessary. And be sure to step back and observe the children's dramatic play. It will tell you a lot about each individual and about the group as a whole. Careful observation and recording will help you gauge the children's interest and figure out how to make your dramatic play area successful.

CHAPTER 9

The Block and Building Area

The block and building area typically contains an assortment of blocks and other items. The other items may include materials such as vehicles, figures, or nature's treasures, to expand the building and play experiences. Often a teacher will rotate the materials, offering the children an opportunity to experience different kinds of building and play.

The block and building area offers young children a variety of learning opportunities. It helps them gain understanding about spatial relationships, cause and effect, arithmetic, physics, and more. Much of this science and math learning occurs through trial and error! The block and building area also offers opportunities for twos and threes to develop sharing skills, learn about boundaries, and explore language. This chapter will give you ideas for making the environment inviting to all—even those who typically do not choose to enter the block and building center.

Setting Up the Block and Building Area

As for all areas in a twos-and-threes classroom, setting up the block and building area requires trial and error to find the materials and the setup that leads to ongoing success. For example, if your current group is fond of making large, spread-out buildings, you may need to move the area around a few times to see what works best. With very young children, the block and building area dynamics change every year.

Consider having blocks always available in your classroom. You can keep blocks readily available on shelves or in bins. Some days you might provide wooden unit blocks, while on other days you might put out alternative blocks such as smaller wooden blocks, larger wooden hollow blocks, Duplo building blocks, foam blocks, and other types of building sets. Adding play items will often bring in children who would not otherwise visit the block area. Here is a list of play items you might provide:

- trucks
- cars
- trains
- people figures
- furniture
- animals
- trees
- road signs
- photos
- books

- planks
- tape measures and rulers
- paper, pencils, and clipboards
- masking tape
- nature items, such as stones, shells, and tree cookies (slices of tree trunks or branches)

- Take pictures of children's structures when you can't leave them standing. Digital photos are helpful for recording what children built, so they can remember and recall something special, for sharing in the block area, or for use in portfolios.

- Encourage group building.

- Take block play outside!

Building and constructing

To store blocks and play items, consider using bins instead of marked shelves for stacking. Bins make cleanup easier. If there is too much emphasis on perfect stacking, cleanup may be overwhelming for two- and three-year-olds. If cleanup is overwhelming, children will be reluctant to cooperate and eventually will feel discouraged from playing in the block and building area. Your main goal should be encouraging children to explore with materials. Focus on getting children—both boys and girls—into the block area, and make cleanup as simple as possible for both children and teachers.

Here are some additional tips for the block and building area:

- Add ethnic diversity in people figures.

- Provide a variety of play items that both girls and boys would like to use.

- Store blocks and play items in clear bins or baskets that are small and light enough for young children to grab and carry.

- Know your comfort zone and establish clear rules. For example, how high will you let the children build? How far may the children carry blocks and accessories away from the block and building area? How long can structures stay standing? How must children show respect for others' structures?

A big building with hollow blocks—outdoors

Hollow blocks and planks outdoors

A big smile in the block area

Your Role

Your main task as an adult managing the block and building area is to keep the play positive and uninterrupted for young children. You need to guide play, encourage children to interact, and foster a positive atmosphere. All these efforts help attract children to the block area.

Children of this age need space to build and explore, as well as space to be alone. Respecting both needs among a group of young children can be difficult. Some children come into the block area loudly and boldly. Their play is simply . . . big! But this can be overwhelming for other children. If the block area is consistently loud and rough, some children will avoid it.

It is important to watch how children use the block area and to note which children use it and which ones avoid it. You may find, for example, that some girls in your group refuse to enter the block area. They might not be interested in blocks or cars. Or perhaps they are nervous about the energy level in that area. Tweaking the materials in the block and building area can entice almost any child. All it takes is creative thinking and really knowing your children.

Let's say you know Hannah loves cats and dogs. You could add a collection of small animals to the building area. You could ask Hannah if she wants to play together with the animals. You could use the blocks for pet kennels, beds, or doghouses. Or perhaps she loves playing house. You could add dollhouse-size babies or housekeeping items and invite other girls and boys to join in the play.

Following are some questions to ask yourself about your block and building area. Use your answers to help you make adjustments and meet the diverse needs of your group.

- How do your children use the area?

- Are some children there more often than others?

- Do some children avoid the area?

- Is the area loud, overwhelming, or geared heavily toward one type of play? For example, does it include only trucks and blocks?

- Does the area contain items that all children enjoy?

- What can you add?

- Do you sit on the floor with children, modeling for them, facilitating play, and giving encouragement?

- Are you careful to protect the space and boundaries of more timid children?

- Would it help to move the block area to a different space in the classroom?

- Can you set up more than one building space and encourage big, loud, bold building outside?

Props with blocks

Safe risk-taking with blocks

Mixing an assortment of blocks

Establishing Rules and Boundaries

Before you try to establish rules and boundaries in your block and building area, think about these key facts:

- Twos and threes need a lot of building space.

- They really enjoy knocking things over, no matter who the builder is.

- Each child will want to use and collect *all* of the materials.

- Twos and threes do not hesitate to take materials from other children.

- They may not yet have the communication skills they need to negotiate. They may lash out to get back what they believe is theirs, cry, and express great frustration.

- Block play modeled for them early on is very important.

- You will need to reiterate your general rules of the block area over and over.

Building a respectful community among egocentric little ones within the small shared space of the block center is hard and important work! It takes perseverance and patience. You must establish ground rules and respect. And you must be present in the block area. You must stay aware of who is building what, understand their intentions and plans, and model negotiation skills. Once the children learn what you model, you will be amazed at what they can do.

Following are some basic rules you might want to start with. While these are simple rules, they still take adult supervision and facilitation to implement. Over time, the children will take ownership of these rules and will respect them.

1. No throwing blocks—that is dangerous.

2. No building things taller than your head unless an adult is helping hold the structure. Blocks falling on heads really hurt.

3. No taking blocks off someone else's structure without asking.

4. No knocking down someone else's structure without permission.

5. Make sure the area is clear before knocking down a structure.

6. If you leave the block area, that says you are all done.

Cardboard and wooden blocks are a good mix.

Saving Structures

Sometimes a child walks away from his or her structure and doesn't look back or show much concern about it. Other children move into the space and play. They may knock down the first child's structure or take pieces off it. Twenty minutes later, the child comes back and claims tearfully, "Hey! That's mine!"

How do you handle this? It's easier if you've laid the ground rules and repeated them frequently using scripts, such as: "If you walk away and are not using the materials, that says you are done, and they are available for the next person."

What about saving structures? Everyone has a different response to this question. You need to decide what feels right to you and other staff in your classroom. Here is how I approach this issue in my classroom. If a child is building a structure and is not done but needs to stop for some reason, then a teacher should ask, "What is your plan?" or "I notice you are leaving. Are you all done building?"

If the answer is yes, then that is that. Once the child walks away, the structure is fair game, and the blocks are open to all. The message is clear and

Add new props regularly.

consistent in my classroom: "If no one is using the blocks, that says they are available." Sometimes this causes tears twenty minutes later when the child returns to find another child using the blocks. But I stick strongly with the consistent message.

Tape and props with blocks

Unit blocks with cars

I work closely with children who don't understand this rule easily. As I see such a child walk away from the blocks, I ask, "Are you sure you are all done using the blocks? If you walk away, that says you are all done, and someone else may take a turn." Often this will bring the child back, saying, "No, no, I'm not done. I'm still using them!"

It's possible this practice may limit the number of children who can be in the block area at once. Sometimes I'll say, "The block area is just a two-person area today. What else do you think you would like to do while you are waiting?" Limiting the number of children who can be in the block area at once is not usually problematic. I find children learn to be respectful of one another's needs.

When the whole group is in transition and we all need to walk away, a child who has been working awhile in the block center may request that the structure not be knocked down or taken apart. When this happens, I will ask the child what his or her plan is. I say, "Okay, let's write a note. What should the note say?" After some early scaffolding, the child replies, "Please don't knock down my blocks." We tape the note beside the block structure for the other children and adults to see. If it's not possible to save the structure—if it's rest time, for example, and we need the space—we will take down the structure. Then, once the block area is back open, that child will get first chance to continue playing there. Sometimes the child runs right back. Sometimes the child is no longer interested.

Treating children's work with respect is very meaningful to the children. It takes time, work, and dialogue to build a community-wide sense of respect.

Very often someone will knock a structure over or steal blocks—even when you are sitting right there. My quickest response is to say, "Hold on . . . ," and then bring back the child who took or knocked down the blocks. I then ask the builder, "Is this okay with you?" Of course, we assume that it's not, but at this age sometimes the answer is yes. But if the answer is no, then we need to rectify the situation. I might say, "So, Nakita, it sounds like Jason was still using those blocks. You will need to give them back." If the blocks were knocked down, I might say, "Nakita, it sounds like Jason was still building here. Let's see if he would like us to help rebuild the castle. Jason, would you like help?" The builder's choice must be respected.

In time, all children within the group will come to know what to expect from the teacher in these situations. Trust must be built between each child and the teacher. The child needs to know the teacher values her words and appreciates her building work, and that the teacher will protect her among the other children. Establishing mutual respect is important. If a teacher were to say only, "We all need to share," the child is likely to feel discouraged and possibly resentful.

Sharing is important, but knowing how to share comes with time. A person must feel "full" before he can give freely. A person learns how to share by having plenty of opportunities to feel "full," to not feel limited to having "just a few," and by experiencing personal time and space to work or play freely.

Write and tape up notes to save structures.

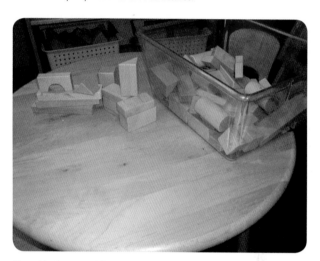

Place blocks on a table to alter the block experience some.

CHAPTER 10

Cooking Experiences and Mealtime Success

Cooking Experiences

Two- and three-year-olds love to cook, bake, and prepare food. They can learn and practice many wonderful skills through cooking, including communicating, taking turns, following directions, measuring and counting ingredients, and learning about good health and healthy food.

It is important to involve children as much as possible in classroom cooking experiences. Read aloud the directions from start to finish. Step-by-step process panels are a must! Keep a camera handy for creating these panels and for documenting the children's work. *Always be alert to food allergies within your group.*

Here are some tips for cooking experiences with very young children:

- Limit the number of children participating to what you can manage successfully.

- Have enough simple jobs for all children in the group to take small turns.

- Allow the children as much responsibility as possible.

- Since prepping is essential, have all materials and ingredients out and available on trays.

A tray prepared in advance

- Divide ingredients or double ingredients if necessary to give all children ample space and the opportunity to participate.

- Provide enough containers, portion cups, and scoops so that children can participate as much as possible.

- Have your camera ready.

- Expect that children will eat some of what they are preparing.

- Don't expect a perfect product. Remember that the process is more important.

- Have baby wipes handy for quick hand cleaning (in case hands go in the mouth or nose) until you can get to a sink.

NO-COOK FOOD PROJECTS

Instant pudding and instant gelatin are easy, fun no-cook projects you could make with your group. You could add fresh fruit to either of these treats. Consider making these two delicious, healthy no-cook snacks with your two- and three-year-olds.

Fruit Salad

Gather all the fruit you would like to use. Wash it thoroughly and put it in small bowls for the children to cut with plastic knives on small cutting boards or paper plates. You will be surprised how capable they are. (Do not be surprised if they eat it as they are cutting!) The children love to use real knives and assist in making their own snack. As the children cut the fruit, they can put it into the big group bowl. Give the fruit another rinse before serving it. After rinsing the fruit, scoop it into a small bowl for each child. Enjoy the fruit salad with fresh cream if you like!

Cutting fruit for a fruit salad

The children love to help.

Graham Cracker Bananas

Slice a few bananas into pieces. Set them aside on a plate. Give each child a sturdy ziplock bag. (Freezer bags work best.) Break one or two graham crackers into quarters and put them into each bag, squeeze out any excess air, and seal the bag. Give each child a small rolling pin. Have the children roll and crunch the graham crackers into crumbs.

Once the crackers are all crumbly, give each child about four banana slices. Have the children drop the bananas into their bags and zip them shut again. They can shake the bags around, coating the bananas with the cracker crumbs. Then they can open the bags and eat the bananas!

COOKING PROJECTS

Cooking projects are an important and well-loved activity in the twos-and-threes classroom. It's important for you to be prepared and to stay focused, because the children enjoy being completely involved in the cooking process. And they love to sample what they have helped cook and bake—an essential finale to the process! Here are a few of my classroom favorites.

Homemade Pizzas

Children really enjoy making their own pizzas. To do this cooking project, you'll need packaged refrigerated biscuit dough. For example, the large-size Pillsbury Grands! biscuits make perfect individual pizzas. The smaller biscuits work well for snack-size pizzas. You could also use English muffins or bagels.

Sprinkling cheese on a homemade pizza

Tape waxed paper to the table and brush it with a bit of oil so the dough does not stick to it. Let the children roll, stretch, and pat the biscuit dough to flatten it out. They may need help. Then give each child a small bowl of sauce and a spoon, as well as a cup of shredded cheese. You can offer other toppings, too, if you like. Remind the children that the ingredients are for the pizza—but expect them to take bites. It is too tempting not to!

Applesauce

Making applesauce is a great project for children to be involved in. Depending on your comfort level and how many adults are available to help, you can have the children fully involved from start to finish, or you can do the peeling yourself.

Set up two workstations when you make applesauce: a peeling station and a cutting station. If possible, use a peeler that clamps to a table. This type of peeler will both peel and core an apple when you turn the crank. The children love turning the crank and peeling the apples all by themselves. The table peeler requires constant adult supervision, though, as it could cut a little finger.

Peeling an apple for applesauce

Cutting apples for applesauce

At the cutting station, provide small cutting boards or paper plates and small plastic knives. Let the children cut the peeled apples on their own. You will probably need to recut the pieces before cooking the apples. It's a good idea to rinse them too.

Once all the apple pieces are ready, put them in a slow cooker, plug it in, and turn it on. Add a bit of water, a tiny bit of sugar, and a sprinkle of cinnamon if you like. Cook the apples right in the classroom if possible so the children can smell the delightful aroma of simmering apples all day! Check the apples often and mash them up a bit. Many children do not like chunky applesauce.

Scrambled Eggs

Scrambled eggs and toast make a homey, comforting snack. Children enjoy helping crack and cook the eggs. Proper sanitation must be practiced, of course—including washing hands thoroughly and immediately, and ensuring that children do not put hands to their mouths when handling raw eggs. Have small bowls for cracking the eggs individually if the children are helping crack them. This will allow you to pick out any stray eggshells easily. Then let the children beat the eggs with a wire whisk or hand-cranked eggbeater.

Whisking the eggs for scrambled eggs

Pancakes and French Toast

Making pancakes can be as simple as using a boxed mix or making more complicated homemade pancakes. If you make pancakes from scratch, you can use nutritious whole-wheat flour or add fresh fruit to the batter. Children love silver dollar–size pancakes, as well as Mickey Mouse–shaped pancakes (one large circle with two small circles for ears). French toast is another wonderful morning snack that children enjoy making and eating.

Cupcakes

If you have a tasty, easy recipe for homemade cupcakes, go for it! Or make it simple and use a boxed mix instead.

Try making vanilla cupcakes topped with fresh whipped cream and sliced strawberries. The children can participate fully in the entire process. First, have them collect all the materials and ingredients, including plenty of small pouring containers. Read all the directions aloud to the children and let them pour in each item. The children can stir the batter with large spoons, wire whisks, or hand-cranked eggbeaters. The children can then scoop the batter into the cupcake liners using scoops or measuring cups.

After the cupcakes have been baked and cooled, portion out frosting in small cups. Give each child a cup of frosting and a plastic knife or clean wooden craft stick. Let the children frost their own cupcakes. Individual containers for frosting are important—it is very tempting to taste the sweet stuff! The containers will keep the children from spreading germs.

Mixing the cupcake batter

Making biscuits from scratch

Frosting the cupcakes

- Cookies: Try making a simple butter cookie or sugar cookie recipe. These have few ingredients and are easy for children to make from scratch.

Stirring the batter for gingerbread cookies

Other Easy Cooking Projects

- Pies: Making pie with young children is a fun and rewarding project. You can make either individual pies in small tins or one or two large pies (depending on the size of your group). If rolled piecrust is too intimidating to make from scratch, make a graham-cracker crust or simply use a premade crust.

- Biscuits: You can make biscuits, like pancakes and cupcakes, from a boxed mix or from scratch. Children love making and eating biscuits with jelly or jam, butter, fresh fruit, and so on.

- Cinnamon rolls: Who doesn't like cinnamon rolls? Homemade cinnamon rolls are a fun project, but they take quite a bit of work, time, and adult assistance. If you would like to make rolls and have the children work more independently, try packaged refrigerated cinnamon roll dough instead.

Making homemade cinnamon rolls

- Corn on the cob: Let the children help husk the corn and explore the ears before they cook and eat them. You might want to do this outdoors at a clean sensory table. Keep the cornhusks and silks at the table through the day for the children to touch and manipulate. They may try to eat the corn raw. This is safe as long as you wash it thoroughly. After the children are done exploring the corn, break the ears in half and cook them. Enjoy as a warm snack!

Husking corn

Successful Mealtimes with Twos and Threes

Group mealtimes are important for twos and threes. Children need experience in order to master eating cooperatively.

At age two or three, children may be having their first experience of sharing meals with other young children. Some children just jump right in and follow along. Other children may need time to adjust.

Many factors play into this transition. Here are some factors that could lead to a more difficult transition:

- lack of experience in a group setting

- being an only child

- cultural differences

- lack of family meals or family time at home

- hurried schedules

- split families

- mealtimes not a priority at home

- special needs

- medical issues

At the beginning of the school year, during the transition into group mealtimes, families may notice a decrease in eating. This is typical. It often passes as the child settles in and adjusts to the new environment.

WHY ARE MEALTIMES SO IMPORTANT?

Mealtime in a twos-and-threes classroom is a pivotal experience. Mealtime helps children learn many social and self-help skills. Here are some of the benefits:

- Mealtimes offer children an opportunity to recognize their names and find their assigned spaces.

- Mealtimes help children develop self-help skills, such as serving themselves, asking for what they need, and tending to various mealtime tasks.

- Mealtimes encourage cooperation. If teachers set the table thoughtfully, they can encourage children to pass things (napkins, water, snack dishes, and so on) to one another.

- Mealtimes help children initiate conversations with one another, be aware when others are speaking, and take turns speaking.

- Mealtimes help children build their language skills.

- Mealtimes introduce the concept of table manners and slowly and subtly help children learn them (being aware of others, staying in your seat until it is time to get up and others are done, covering your mouth, saying please and thank you, and so on).

- Mealtimes help children practice following directions, cleaning up, and packing up.

- Mealtimes build a sense of classroom community.

MEALTIMES IN MY CLASSROOM

In my room, I use a careful and thoughtful plan for mealtimes. I do not fuss about manners at the beginning of the school year. Instead, we focus more on joining together as a group, learning to become aware of and thoughtful toward others, and learning to engage in conversations by showing interest in what others are saying and waiting for our turn to speak. These skills take time and practice to develop.

I slowly begin focusing on appropriate table manners. We practice saying polite mealtime phrases, such as "Please pass the juice," and "Thank you!" I arrange the table in a way that encourages children to pass items to one another. It is easier for them to pour and pass, and more spills and shouting initially occur when children do these tasks on

their own, but the benefits of developing independence outweigh the challenges!

Typically, I encourage children to be more independent in serving themselves, passing items, and pouring food a few months into the school year. I provide a photo-sequence chart to help them. This chart serves several purposes. It provides a visual model of expectations, which is important for all children—particularly younger children and children with special needs. It also provides a beautiful way to develop literacy and sequencing skills. I make a new chart each year with photos of the current children. Seeing themselves in the chart attracts the children's interest and helps them learn.

I try to time the switch from sippy cups to pitchers and small open cups as we begin our curriculum unit on food and restaurants. Our discussions turn toward trying different kinds of food, making healthy food choices, having meals together, eating in restaurants, getting served, serving others, playing roles, using manners, and deciding what you like and don't like. The transition happens subtly as part of the flow of the curriculum.

Desserts can cause controversy in the classroom. Some teachers have this rule: "You need to eat your grow food first then your dessert." I have thought about this message intently throughout the years. In my early days, I followed suit. But then I began to ask myself: "Why am I presenting children with this message?" It is a message that often leads to tears and power struggles. Younger children think, "I see it in my lunch box. That means it is mine, and I want it." If families are sending in lunch boxes, I encourage them to send in healthy foods, and I explain to them that I will not control the order in which children eat the food.

I began looking at desserts from a different perspective. I began assuming that if families pack desserts for lunch, they are telling their children and the teachers that the dessert is fine to eat. The order should not matter if the family says it is a healthy choice. Dictating, "Eat this first, and then that," is not the teacher's responsibility.

I believe it's important for children to make choices at the lunch table. If families don't want their children to eat a dessert first, then I suggest to them early in the year that they save desserts for dinnertime. I reassure them that I don't mean to be disrespectful. I simply want to respect the children's independence, develop their ability to make good decisions, avoid power struggles, and promote positive food experiences within the group. Often, even when children eat dessert first, they come back to the healthy food afterward. I don't believe it is appropriate to use bribes and coercion in the classroom—especially around meals and food. The food a child eats is closely linked to his or her developing sense of comfort, security, and self-esteem.

Some days a child may be upset, may want something more or less, or may want what another child has. In these cases, we write a note to the family and put it in the child's lunch box. The note is in the child's words. I start with "Dear..." and then ask, "What would you like the note to say?" The child may reply, "Mommy, I want more yogurt," or "I didn't like my pasta. I want peanut butter."

YOUR ROLE

We as teachers need to be mindful of our role in meals with young children. We must model healthy and positive eating habits not only for the children themselves but also for their families. Following are some tips to help you be an effective mealtime model:

- Sit down with the children; don't hover over them.

- Talk in a soft, calm voice, and encourage the same from the children.

- Keep adult discussions to a minimum.

- Be mindful of all allergies, special needs, and choking hazards. Carefully plan seating of individuals with special food needs for maximum safety.

- Try to be proactive and well prepared for the meal to limit the amount of standing up and sitting down.

- Try to promote slow, peaceful eating. Teach children to enjoy the company of others and the food they are eating.

- Discourage silliness at the lunch table. Being silly is fun, but with twos and threes, silliness can quickly escalate to chaos, which can raise the risk of choking. It can also be too loud for certain children.

- Establish your eating philosophy and rules with families at the start of the school year.

To encourage young children to eat their food while still having fun, try these mealtime games:

- Play I Spy: "I spy with my little eye... someone's food that is... green!"

- Recite nursery rhymes, taking a bite between rhymes.

- Play a guessing game about what a child will bite next. For example: "I think you will bite... chicken!"

- Tell very short stories, taking a bite between stories.

- Play a rhyming game with food words. For example: "*Ham* rhymes with *Sam*. *Bread* rhymes with *red*."

- Chant a turn-taking rhyme, such as "Bubble Gum, Bubble Gum," "Engine, Engine Number Nine," or "Eeny, Meeny, Miny, Mo." While saying the chant, point to each food choice. Whatever you're pointing to on the last word, that is the bite to eat. For example: "Bubble gum, bubble gum in a dish. Tell me which food do you wish?... Carrots!"

CHAPTER 11

Field Trips and Special Events

Adding an additional layer to your program with field trips and special events is exciting, and both are well worth the efforts involved. Finding what suits your program, what resources you have available, and what support you have will help you to start the planning process. This chapter will provide you with a handful of ideas for field trips and special onsite events, as well as some tips for worry-free excursions.

Field Trips

Field trips offer many benefits to two- and three-year-olds. Outings give children an opportunity to see new, different, and interesting locations, things, and people. They offer a change of pace from the daily routine. They extend classroom learning out into the world. They offer new hands-on experiences not available in the classroom. They provide new information from experienced, knowledgeable, and passionate people. They give children a chance to connect with—and sometimes serve—the community.

Taking other people's children on excursions away from your school, center, or home is a big responsibility. You should consider many things before committing to an excursion. Here are some questions to consider:

- What is available in your area?

- What is accessible within walking distance?

- What is in close range for driving?

- What are the interests of your current group?

- What type of excursion would mesh well with your curriculum?

- What would make a good trip for a short period of time?

- What type of plan do you feel comfortable carrying out?

- How much adult help do you have?

Early in the year, when you're welcoming new families, ask if they are interested in sharing their skills, interests, and availability by planning or chaperoning field trips. You may be surprised at how interested and willing families are to help. Some people simply cannot take time off from work for such events, but others can—and would love to.

....

For several years in a row, I took my children to a local sheep farm. It was a delightful trip to see the sheep, visit the small pond, take a hayride, and eat our lunches in the family's home. One year a particular child was beside himself with excitement over just sitting on top of a tractor. He would have been satisfied if that had been the entire field trip!

....

Be creative in your planning. Develop field trip ideas based on both your resources and your limitations. And don't forget to consider your curriculum.

Field trip ideas often grow from curriculum themes or concepts children are learning. For example, if your children are learning about baby animals, a farm visit would be a great field trip. If your children are learning about a wide variety of wild animals, a trip to a nearby zoo is a great follow-up. If your children are learning basic science concepts, consider visiting the nearest children's museum.

Here are some excursion ideas to consider:

- picnic at an interesting, out-of-the-ordinary place

- picking apples, pumpkins, strawberries, or other fruits according to season

- farm visit (dairy farm, horse farm, vegetable farm, and so on)

- petting zoo

- local zoo

- children's museum

- pizza restaurant

- ice scream stand, shop, or restaurant

- park

- library

- short train or bus ride

- miniature golf course

- bookstore that offers children's story time

- bakery

- greenhouse

- farmers' market

- art gallery

- pet store

- aquarium

- nursing home

- science museum

- any natural setting

- local construction site (viewed from a safe distance)

And here are several tips for successful field trips:

- Before taking your children someplace new, visit the setting on your own to make sure it is truly appropriate and safe and to get familiar with it. (For example, find out where the toilets are!)

- Find out the site's rules in advance and prepare the children for these rules ahead of time.

- Call your destination well in advance to ensure that the date you want to visit is available. Then call to confirm the week before your visit. Miscommunications and booking errors can be disastrous when discovered at the last moment!

- Plan your outing carefully from beginning to end. Don't make the trip too long. Consider how timing may affect lunch or rest time.

- Invite the children's family members to join your outing.

- Make sure you have the proper child-adult ratio.

- Have permission slips, children's emergency cards, and allergy alerts with you.

- Carry a backpack containing a first aid kit, spare clothes, extra diapers, tissues, baby wipes, ziplock bags and plastic grocery bags, pens, paper, black permanent markers, and spare water bottles.

- Bring water and snacks (or lunch if appropriate) for each child.

- Have a rain plan.

- Keep a good head count. Count and recount throughout the trip!

- Use a buddy system.

- Have name tags for children. Stick the tags on their backs so the children will not peel them off. Put your name or your center or school's name and phone number on the label.

- Consider making matching brightly colored or tie-dyed shirts for all the children to wear during the field trip. Matching shirts will help you keep an eye on everyone.

- Expect things to go wrong, and have a backup plan.

- Have a spare activity ready, such as a book to read, small notepads for drawing, and so on.

- Strategically place children with chaperones who will be the best fit for their needs.

- Keep children with challenging behaviors or anxieties with you or your coteacher.

- If you have a large group of children, divide them into groups with color-coded name tags. Give each group's chaperone the same color name tag and a card with all the children's names on it.

- Take lots of photos.

- Be a good conversationalist.

- Have fun!

Onsite Guests and Special Events

Taking children on field trips is great fun, but outings are not always possible. Limiting circumstances may include financial restraints, lack of adult participation, or geographical disadvantages. What can you do to broaden children's experiences when it is too difficult to take children offsite?

Plan onsite special events or bring in special guests! As with field trips, let your curriculum and your resources inspire your special events and guests. Solicit families for ideas and talents they might be willing to share!

A visit from the local fire department

Here are some special event ideas to consider:

- Make a pumpkin patch for pumpkin picking.

- Decorate or spruce up an area to resemble a field trip you'd like to take.

- Bring in animals.

- Have a water fun day.

- Have a sports day.

- Have a carnival.

- Have a parade.

- Have picnics!

  And here are some ideas for guest speakers:

- veterinarian

- doctor

- farmer

- construction worker

- parent with a baby

- someone who works with food, such as a chef or baker

- someone who gardens

- dog trainer

- music and movement specialist

- musician

- artist

- clown

- chemist, engineer, or other science professional

- any family members willing to share their talents

. . . .

One year for a special guest visit, I invited an artist to come and paint in our classroom with professional materials. I used this experience to introduce the children to canvas painting. I borrowed easels from other classrooms and moved furniture to make our classroom into a large art studio so all the children could paint at once!

. . . .

Final Thoughts

I hope this book has helped you see two- and three-year-olds with delight. This is a special age—one like no other. When you spend a year with a child who is between two and three years old, you witness a spectacular unfolding!

I also hope this book has inspired you to give twos and threes many opportunities to experience connection, joy, and wonder in your program. You can truly make a difference in the children's lives. You help guide each child through so many first experiences, and you help form the foundations of relationships, independence, literacy, and much, much more.

Teaching young children is a profound experience—not one to be taken lightly. But you still need to remember to be in the moment with children, enjoying all the giggles and hugs along the way. Being in the moment will help you build relationships. And a warm relationship with each child and family is critical to a successful year.

I have dedicated my life to young children, and I have no regrets about this choice. I wish for you the same passion in your work.

Be true to your values and your beliefs. Always put children first. Be their best advocate! Thank you for striving to be the best you can be for children—and for teaching children to be the best they can be.

Advice for Every
Early Childhood Educator

1

Work hard.

2

Laugh a lot!

Eat well, and treat yourself to something special every now and then.

Don't forget to take breaks and rest well.

Read a good book or website for ideas.

6

Carefully plan your
curriculum with
each child in mind.

7

Know that sometimes you
have to throw your plan away
and follow a child's lead.

8

Take many photos and notes.

9

Learn to see what children see.

10

Be silly sometimes and enjoy
every moment with children.

11

Nurture friendships.

12

Take risks and encourage children
to safely take risks as well.

13

Help children explore
the natural world.

14

Take children outdoors.

15

Savor quiet moments.

16

Stop yourself from saying no.
Find out what a child's plan is first.

17

Build loving relationships,
and love with all your heart!

Appendixes

Weekly Curriculum Planning Sheet Template

DATE:

WEEKLY THEME:

	MONDAY	TUESDAY	WEDNESDAY	THURSDAY	FRIDAY
SENSORY TABLE					
MANIPULATIVE					
WRITING TABLE					
BLOCK AREA					
DRAMATIC PLAY					
GATHERING					

					WHAT WORKED, DIDN'T WORK, OR THINGS I WOULD CHANGE:
				NOTES:	
				SETUP:	
				BOOKS:	
SNACK	TEXTURE TABLE	ART	EASEL	ITEMS TO PURCHASE:	REFLECTIONS:

Weekly Curriculum Planning Sheet Example #1

DATE: November 3–7

WEEKLY THEME: Construction: (Vehicles) week one

	MONDAY	TUESDAY	WEDNESDAY	THURSDAY	FRIDAY
SENSORY TABLE	Playdough w/ rollers, cutters	Sand on trays w/ small construction vehicles	Gak w/ cutters, scissors	Dirt on trays w/ vehicles, brooms	Playdough w/ hammers and golf tees
MANIPULATIVE	Construction puzzles	Construction magnet set	Lacing spool set	Gear set	Duplo set on table w/ trays for building
WRITING TABLE	Yellow/black booklets w/ vehicle stickers, pencils	Small clipboards w/ colored pencils	Large chalkboards w/ sidewalk chalk	Large clipboards w/ carpenter pencils	Whiteboards w/ markers, small sponges
BLOCK AREA	Hollow blocks, open building	Black road set w/ medium vehicles	Unit blocks w/ vehicles	Duplo building set	Little Tikes road set w/ trucks and people
DRAMATIC PLAY	Construction work zone: workbench, tools, hard hats, aprons, play phones, keys, clipboards, pencils, rulers, keyboard, "desk," ride-on trucks (stationary), mini lunch boxes, bags for gathering items, tool pouch, etc.				
GATHERING	Intro to "Construction"	"Drive, Drive, Drive the Truck" song	Book: "On the Job"	Vehicle match game	"What's missing" game: vehicles

SNACK	Cereal with milk	Cinnamon bread	Make our own pizzas!	Cheese and apple slices	Scrambled eggs
TEXTURE TABLE	Water, bubbles, scrubbers, plastic vehicles	Sand w/ vehicles, scoopers	Sand w/ vehicles, brooms, mini rakes	Water, funnels, bottles, scoops, etc.	Dirt w/ vehicles, scrappers, mini shovels
ART	Spin art	Mini easels (black, white, yellow, orange)	Texture painting, sand in paint, mix as desire	Group painting for foamy paint	Tire print painting
EASEL	Wet chalk on black paper	Crayons with colored paper	Bingo stampers	Silky crayons	Paint cups

ITEMS TO PURCHASE:
More golf tees, construction stickers

SETUP: Gather the dramatic play items.

BOOKS: Order books from library.

NOTES:
Look for LARGE box for house for next week!

REFLECTIONS:
The box "Truck" project worked out great. We used it with the sit-on wheel as a truck back. The "workers" loaded, unloaded, and reloaded the large and hollow blocks.

WHAT WORKED, DIDN'T WORK, OR THINGS I WOULD CHANGE:
Get 2 more small clipboards. 2 are missing and conflict arose with only 2 available.

Weekly Curriculum Planning Sheet Example #2

DATE: September 27–October 1

WEEKLY THEME: BABIES!

	MONDAY	TUESDAY	WEDNESDAY	THURSDAY	FRIDAY
SENSORY TABLE	Playdough w/ cutters	Salt on trays w/ zoo animals	Playdough w/ Mr. Potato Head pieces	Gak w/ scissors and cutters	Playdough w/ ovens, pretend candles, rollers
MANIPULATIVE	Puzzles	Baby magnet set	"Whose Baby?" match set	Animal lacing cards	Peg w/ tray set
WRITING TABLE	Booklets w/ stickers, thin markers	Full sheet of paper w/ silky crayons	Sketch paper w/ new charcoal pencils	Small clipboards w/ pencils	Large writing table w/ scissors, tape, etc.
BLOCK AREA	Unit blocks, open building	Rainbow blocks w/ family set	"Quint" family baby set w/ small wooden blocks	Small wooden blocks (quint set if interested)	Unit blocks w/ ponies, baby ponies
DRAMATIC PLAY	Baby nursery: baby cradle/sink, ALL baby dolls, baby bed, baby high chair, bibs, baby food, baby potty chair, pretend lotions, baby bottles, diapers, blankets, soft pillows, baby doll clothes, bags for carrying items, rattles, strollers, etc.				
GATHERING	Intro "Babies" unit	"Kiss the Baby Good Night" song	"Rock-a-Bye Baby." Bring out chart from taster test.	Intro class "I Used to Be a Baby" book w/ their pictures/words.	"What's Missing?" game (baby items)

SNACK	Cereal with milk, bananas	Baby food taste test (chart: like/not like)	Fresh fruit	Make homemade muffins early w/ kids	Oatmeal w/ blueberries
TEXTURE TABLE	Colored rice, small babies, nesting cups	Bubble water, small babies, mini washcloths	Water, large babies, small sponges, towels to dry, scoops	Lentils, mini pots, pans, scoops, etc.	Color tinted water, baby bottles, scoops, funnels, etc.
ART	Bubble prints	Fingerpainting	Soft collage	Poster board, paint w/ rollers, wide brushes, day 1, darker colors	Poster board cont. light colors, regular brushes
EASEL	Silky crayons	Pastel paint cups w/ large paper	Pastel paint w/ rollers and large paper	New sidewalk chalk (add water if they want wet)	Black paper w/ thin brushes and bright paint

ITEMS TO PURCHASE:
Baby food, baby cookies

SETUP: Baby nursery in dramatic play

BOOKS: Gather books, pick up new from library.

NOTES:

REFLECTIONS:

- They were so incredibly sweet with the "Kiss the Baby" song. The mini blankets I made for the song were a BIG hit for the children. It added a real gentle touch with the tiny dolls.
- The dramatic play nursery was HUGE! More children entered this week.
- The transformation of the block area worked really well. Everyone was interested in joining.

WHAT WORKED, DIDN'T WORK, OR THINGS I WOULD CHANGE:

- Put the poster board out next week with silky crayons and oil pastels. See how they do with it. We can either leave as is at that point or see if they want to add collage materials. It looks really cool right now.
- Make sure next year we only get the exact baby food we ask for. The children DEF do not like the vegetables!

Weekly Curriculum Planning Sheet Example #3

DATE: April 28–May 1

WEEKLY THEME: Butterflies

	MONDAY	TUESDAY	WEDNESDAY	THURSDAY	FRIDAY
SENSORY TABLE	Playdough w/ cutters	Goop w/ color tray and eyedroppers	Gak w/ markers, scissors, cutters	Dirt, plastic insects, scoops, mini rakes	Playdough, mini silk flowers w/ stems, plastic butterflies
MANIPULATIVE	Insect puzzles	Peg and hammer set	"Who's Home?" matching lotto game	Lacing cards: shapes	Magnet books
WRITING TABLE	Mini clipboards, carpenter pencils	Science table—cocoons (then move to science shelf)	Pastel booklets w/ colored pencils, stickers	Whiteboards w/ markers	Large full sheet w/ assorted mediums
BLOCK AREA	Unit blocks, add insect basket, nature basket	Duplo building set	Train set	Large foam road set, car, mini blocks	Unit blocks, insect basket, nature basket
DRAMATIC PLAY	Pond accessories, flowers, bench, nature items, gardening items, science items, soft pillows, scarves, mini books				
GATHERING	Intro: "Butterflies"	"I Wanna Be a Butterfly" song	Big book: "A Butterfly Is Born"	Lifecycle: Butterflies	"What's Missing?" game

SNACK	"Birthday snack"	Yogurt w/ granola	Cereal w/ milk and bananas	Pancakes	Biscuits made yesterday
TEXTURE TABLE	Butterflies, scoops, rice	Peas, silk flower petals, scoops	Nature table from hike	Nature table with caterpillars (fake)	Water w/ frogs, lily pads, scoops
ART	Mini easels, thin brushes	Papier-mâché cocoons	Fold art	Paint papier-mâché cocoons	Group large box marble painting
EASEL	Large crayons, colored paper	Spool painting	Paint cups w/ large paper	Oil pastels w/ watercolors	Rainbow crayons

ITEMS TO PURCHASE:

SETUP:

NOTES:
Have butterfly house set up and ready

BOOKS: butterfly books, life cycle, insects

REFLECTIONS:
- Look into new life-cycle collection books.
- Order new life-cycle butterfly set since it appears the "chrysalis" is missing.

WHAT WORKED, DIDN'T WORK, OR THINGS I WOULD CHANGE:
Rethink science area for this unit. How to bring it together more with other areas of the room.

Weekly Curriculum Planning Sheet Example #4

DATE: February 27–March 4

WEEKLY THEME: Storybook Favorites: "Goldilocks and the Three Bears"

	MONDAY	TUESDAY	WEDNESDAY	THURSDAY	FRIDAY
SENSORY TABLE	Playdough w/ rollers, cutters	Oats, bears, scoops	Gak w/ bear cutters and bear stampers	Playdough w/ bears, "Goldilocks" (and mini houses)	Goop w/ colors and eyedroppers
MANIPULATIVE	Bear puzzles	Bear match car set	Dress-up bears	Cookie, cake sorter sets	Lacing card set
WRITING TABLE	Small clipboards w/ pencils	White paper w/ brown mediums	Full writing table w/ scissors, tape, etc.	Booklets w/ stickers, thin markers	Mini chalkboards
BLOCK AREA	Duplo "Family" set	2 soft houses w/ bear families; add "Goldilocks"	Unit blocks, bear families	Hollow blocks— open building	Zoo pets w/ unit blocks
DRAMATIC PLAY	Housekeeping, play food, 3 chairs, 3 beds, 3 bowls, soft pillows, 2 children's rocking chairs, play food, soft and stuffed bears				
GATHERING	Intro: "Goldilocks & the Three Bears"	Flannel board story	Finger puppets for story	Story told with figures and houses	Act out story

SNACK	Mini bagels with cream cheese	Fruit with Teddy Grahams	Oatmeal w/ strawberries	Apples w/ peanut butter	Pancakes
TEXTURE TABLE	Rice, counting bears	Water, bear family	Oats, bowls, spoons	Oats, bears, girl figures, mini chairs	Water, pots, pans, bubbles, sponges
ART	Monoprinting	Papa Bear's bed: sculpture	Mama Bear's bed: sculpture	Baby Bear's bed: sculpture	Artist's choice
EASEL	Paint cups (shades of brown)	Roller spool painting	Brayers w/ shades of brown	Brown paper w/ white and black paint	Silky crayons

ITEMS TO PURCHASE:

SETUP: Get BIG box for bear cave to paint.

BOOKS: Order books.

NOTES:
*Order books for next week, "Three Little Pigs."

REFLECTIONS:
- I think we will continue acting out story in the afternoons next week. I think we can stretch out this unit with interest still from the children.
- I ordered new set of Goldilocks characters for next year.

WHAT WORKED, DIDN'T WORK, OR THINGS I WOULD CHANGE:
This unit was well received. I think everything went well.

Weekly Curriculum Planning Sheet Example #5

DATE: January 24–28

WEEKLY THEME: Nursery Rhymes (week one)

	MONDAY	TUESDAY	WEDNESDAY	THURSDAY	FRIDAY
SENSORY TABLE	Playdough w/ cutters	Salt w/ scoops and scrapers	Dirt on trays, trucks, brooms, etc.	Gak, mini plastic eggs, cutters, scissors	Goop w/ eyedroppers and colors
MANIPULATIVE	Lacing spools	Matching bears set	Mice shape sorting set	Mini castle block set	Puzzles
WRITING TABLE	Chalk and chalkboards	Booklets w/ stickers, colored pencils	Full sheet of paper taped on table w/ tape, oil pastels	Clipboards w/ large pencils	Full table w/ markers, scissors, tape, etc.
BLOCK AREA	Farm animals added to block area	Dogs added to block area	Train set	Unit blocks w/ castle, figures, and plastic eggs	Hollow blocks
DRAMATIC PLAY	Beanie Babies, play dishes, cupboard, soft pillows, rocking chairs, baskets of small books, "Humpty" eggs, aprons, shape clock, small basket of dishes and food, etc.				
GATHERING	Today's rhyme: "Hey, Diddle Diddle"	Today's rhyme: "Old Mother Hubbard"	Today's rhyme: "Hickory Dickory Dock"	Today's rhyme: "Humpty Dumpty"	Today's rhyme: "Jack and Jill"

SNACK	Cereal w/ milk, bananas	English muffins	Yogurt and fruit	Mini bagels w/ cream cheese	Cheese and crackers
TEXTURE TABLE	Water, scoops, waterwheels	Lentils, dogs, people	Rice, mice, scoops	Castle set (move from morning), rice, eggs	Bubble water, small pails, scoops, funnels
ART	Marble painting	Old Mother Hubbard's cupboard box sculpture	Cardboard w/ texture brushes	Eggshell collage	Spray painting at easel
EASEL	Tempera cake watercolors	Paint cups w/ thin brushes	Markers w/ paper	Chalk in holders (wet and dry)	Spray painting (also outside in snow)

ITEMS TO PURCHASE:
New spray bottles from dollar store

SETUP: Nursery Rhyme collection

BOOKS:

NOTES:
If snow day Friday, push "Jack and Jill" to Monday.

REFLECTIONS:
The unit has started off great. I can see this group enjoying it for the full four weeks. But we will see how it goes.

WHAT WORKED, DIDN'T WORK, OR THINGS I WOULD CHANGE:
- I need to find my extra baskets with handles. The children in this group enjoy carrying the small rhyme books in the baskets. There are not enough to go around. If I can't find by next week, I will go to Michael's to get more.
- Without the wall space, I should make book with each nursery rhyme finished to have collection for the children to look through and recall.

Weekly Curriculum Planning Sheet Example #6

DATE: January 14–18

WEEKLY THEME: Storybook Favorites: *The Mitten by Jan Brett*

	MONDAY	TUESDAY	WEDNESDAY	THURSDAY	FRIDAY
SENSORY TABLE	White playdough w/ assorted cutters	White gak w/ animals	Salt, forest animals, trees, brooms	Playdough w/ animal cutters	Shaving cream w/ colored sticks, eyedroppers w/ color
MANIPULATIVE	Shape sorter set	Animal puzzles	Lock box w/ animals inside	Cookie shape sorters	"Feely" box
WRITING TABLE	Small chalkboards w/ chalk	Large clipboards	Full writing table w/ scissors, tape, thin markers, pencils	Real drawing paper w/ charcoal pencils	Stampers, crayons
BLOCK AREA	Hollow blocks	Hollow blocks w/ animals	Unit blocks w/ animals	Train set	Builder's choice
DRAMATIC PLAY	Fake snow felt, real logs, mittens, boots, winter scarves, beanie animals, "forest branches," nature items, housekeeping items, play food.				
GATHERING	Intro: "The Mitten" book	Books and tape: "The Mitten" song: "Two Warm Mittens"	Flannel set: "The Mitten"	Large mitten, character figures w/ story	Act out!

SNACK	Toast w/ apple butter	Animal crackers w/ raisins	Pasta w/ parmesan cheese	Cereal w/ milk, strawberries	Bagels w/ cream cheese
TEXTURE TABLE	White rice, forest animals	Snow w/ forest animals	Snow w/ mittens, shovels	Snow w/ construction vehicles	Bubble water, waterwheels, scoops
ART	White-item collage	Group painting w/ texture mittens	Paint large box for "bear cave"	Glue items on bear cave	Make marbled prints from shaving cream
EASEL	White foam painting	New scented pencils	(Try) condensed milk painting at easel	Large crayons w/ big paper	Blue/black paper w/ white mediums

ITEMS TO PURCHASE:
Snack items above

SETUP: Dramatic play (forest/house)

BOOKS: 2 copies of "The Mitten," snow books, forest animals, winter, etc.

NOTES:
Get large box by Tuesday for bear cave.

REFLECTIONS:
- The children loved the story!
- Next time we should act out in the big room.
- Have someone available to help X.
- X needed support as well.
- We had hoped for shaving cream this week, but we did not have the appropriate staff this week.

WHAT WORKED, DIDN'T WORK, OR THINGS I WOULD CHANGE:
Get more "squirt" bottles!!!!

Weekly Curriculum Planning Sheet Example #7

DATE: September 5–9

WEEKLY THEME: Welcome to School

	MONDAY	TUESDAY	WEDNESDAY	THURSDAY	FRIDAY
SENSORY TABLE	Playdough w/ small ovens, rollers, etc.	Playdough w/ rollers and cookie cutters	Sand on trays w/ small vehicles and brooms	Playdough w/ small ovens, rollers, and cutters	Playdough w/ stampers, cutters
MANIPULATIVE	Simple puzzles	Large peg set	Farm magnet set	Peg set w/ mats and bowls	Simple puzzles
WRITING TABLE	Colored paper w/ colored pencils	Mini chalkboards w/ chalk in holders	Booklets w/ crayons, stickers	White paper w/ rainbow crayons	Large chalkboard w/ sidewalk chalk
BLOCK AREA	Small unit blocks, people figures, cars	Small unit blocks, people figures	Train set	Train set	Unit blocks, construction vehicles
DRAMATIC PLAY	Housekeeping, table and chairs, pots and pans, dishes, play food, baby dolls, high chair, baby bed, baby blankets, small bags for collecting and carrying, telephones, play keys, cameras, and soft Beanie animals				
GATHERING	Welcome to School	"Twinkle, Twinkle, Little Star"	"Old MacDonald Had a Farm"	"Five Little Ducks"	"The Wheels on the Bus"

SNACK	Grahams and bananas	Goldfish and raisins	Yogurt w/ strawberries	Pretzels w/ applesauce	Crackers and cheese
TEXTURE TABLE	Water, funnels, scoopers	Water, small babies, bubbles	Sand, mini shovels, mini molds	Water, rubber ducks	Sand, vehicles, small shovels
ART	Bingo stampers w/ large paper	Large cardboard group painting w/ tempera watercolors	Oil pastels, watercolors, continue project	Collage w/ materials	Group large roll paper w/ rollers and paint
EASEL	Large paper w/ large crayons	Bingo stampers	Sidewalk chalk in holders	Paint cups w/ large paper	Markers w/ large paper

ITEMS TO PURCHASE:
Snack items

SETUP: Simple

BOOKS: Board books, familiar

NOTES:
*Make sure enough coverage for paint at easel.

REFLECTIONS:
- The first week went really well.
- I liked watching the friendship between J and A.
- Make science area more noticeable.
- This group LOVED the yogurt!

WHAT WORKED, DIDN'T WORK, OR THINGS I WOULD CHANGE:
- Markers without continuous supervision.
- Lids went into X's mouth. He also colored hands. Save for another week or so when routines settle or more support is available.

Art and Other Recipes

PAPIER-MÂCHÉ FLOUR MIXTURE

3 parts water
1 part flour
Newspaper strips

Stir water into flour until the paste is smooth and creamy. Dip each strip of newspaper in the paste and apply it one piece at a time to the mold you are using to form your sculpture.

PAPIER-MÂCHÉ GLUE MIXTURE

2 parts white glue
1 part warm water
Newspaper strips

Mix glue with water. Stir well until completely blended. Dip each strip of newspaper in the glue mixture and apply it one piece at a time to the mold you are using to form your desired sculpture.

BUBBLE SOLUTION ONE

⅔ cup liquid dishwashing detergent
1 gallon water
1 tablespoon glycerin

Mix all ingredients together. Store the solution in a covered container. The bubble solution works best after setting for three to five days.

BUBBLE SOLUTION TWO

½ cup liquid dishwashing detergent
4½ cups water
4 tablespoons glycerin

Mix all ingredients together. Store the solution in a covered container. The bubble solution works best after setting for three to five days.

PLAYDOUGH

4 cups boiling water
4 tablespoons vegetable oil
Food coloring
4 cups flour
2 cups salt
2 tablespoons cream of tartar

Mix water, oil, and food coloring in one bowl. Mix flour, salt, and cream of tartar in a separate bowl. Pour wet mixture into dry mixture. Stir together and knead the mixture as it cools. Store the playdough in an airtight container.

NO-COOK PLAYDOUGH

1 cup salt
1½ cups flour
½ cup salt
2 tablespoons oil
Food coloring

Mix all the ingredients thoroughly. Store the playdough in an airtight container.

GAK

12 ounces white glue
12 ounces cold water
4½ tablespoons borax
12 ounces hot water

Mix glue and cold water in one bowl. Mix borax and hot water in a separate bowl. Pour the borax mixture into the glue mixture. Stir until slimy, stringy, rubbery gak forms. Store the gak in a large ziplock bag or an airtight container.

RAINBOW STEW

⅓ cup sugar
1 cup cornstarch
4 cups cold water
Food coloring

Mix the sugar, cornstarch, and water in a large saucepan. Heat this mixture on the stovetop over medium heat, stirring constantly, until it begins to thicken. Set the mixture aside to cool. Divide the cooled mixture into three bowls. Add a different color of food coloring to each bowl and mix it in. Place three heaping tablespoons of each colored mixture in one ziplock bag. Knead the bag to mix the colors into a rainbow stew!

FLUBBER

1 cup white glue
1 cup water
2 teaspoons food coloring or liquid tempera paint
4 tablespoons borax
1⅓ cups warm water

Mix the glue, water, and food coloring or paint together in one bowl. Mix the borax and warm water in a separate bowl until the borax dissolves completely. Then *slowly* pour the glue solution into the borax solution—but *do not mix*. Roll the glue solution around once or twice in the borax solution and then remove glue solution and knead for 2 to 3 minutes.

GOOP

1 part water
2 parts cornstarch
Food coloring (optional)

Add water slowly to cornstarch and stir. The mixture should be solid when you hold it but gooey as you let it drip and ooze down. As the goop dries, you can add more water and stir.

If you want colored goop, add food coloring to the water before mixing the water and cornstarch. If you would like the children to add their own colors, use ice cube trays and eyedroppers to measure out food coloring. Small squirt bottles work well for adding water.

CORN SYRUP PAINT

Corn syrup
Food coloring

Divide one or more bottles of corn syrup evenly among several containers. Add a few drops of a different food coloring to each container and mix. This type of paint dries transparent. It takes a few days to dry.

CONDENSED MILK PAINT

1 can sweetened condensed milk
Food coloring or liquid watercolor paint

Pour the milk into small bowls or containers. Add several drops of food coloring or paint to each dish and stir. Apply paint to thick paper. The painting will dry shiny. It may take a day or two to dry, especially if paint is applied heavily.

SALT PAINT

2 teaspoons salt
1 teaspoon liquid starch
3 to 4 drops food coloring

Mix all the ingredients together. The salt gives a frosted or sandy appearance to the paint.

CRYSTALLIZED PAINTING

2 cups water
2 cups Epsom salts
Food coloring

In a small pot, combine water and Epsom salts. Bring the mixture to a boil. Stir the mixture and then let it cool down. Mix in the food coloring. Paint it onto paper. The paint will be transparent when wet and will dry into colored crystals.

PUFFY PAINT ONE

1 cup salt
1 cup flour
1 cup water
Food coloring or tempera paint

Mix all ingredients together and put the paint in squeeze bottles.

PUFFY PAINT TWO

2 tablespoons tempera paint
⅓ cup white glue
2 cups nonmenthol shaving cream

Mix all ingredients together and put the paint in squeeze bottles. Use this paint soon after making it.

WINDOW PAINT

1½ cups dishwashing detergent
¾ cup cornstarch
Food coloring

Mix the detergent and cornstarch. Divide the mixture into containers according to how many colors you want. Add several drops of coloring to each container and stir until completely mixed.

GRASS HEADS

Old nylon pantyhose
Grass seeds
Sawdust or potting soil
Decorations: googly eyes, yarn, fabric scraps, permanent marker, and so on
Waterproof glue
Small yogurt cup

Cut the pantyhose into stockings about 8 inches long, including the toe portion. Stretch the open end of each stocking over the top of a large cup or mug; leave the toe dangling inside the cup. With a plastic spoon, scoop in about 2 teaspoons of grass seeds. Pack in some sawdust or potting soil to make a clump about the size of a tennis ball. Tie a knot in the open end of the stocking to close it. Decorate the grass head as desired, using googly eyes, yarn, fabric scraps, or permanent marker to create a face and hair. (The toe end of the stocking, where the grass seed is, should be the top of the head.) Dunk the head into a bowl of water to moisten it. Fill the yogurt cup halfway with water. Rest the head on the rim of the cup, with the tied end of the stocking dangling into the water. Put the grass heads on a windowsill or any other place that gets a lot of sunlight. Have the children check every day to make sure the heads are moist, and let them add a small portion of water if needed. The grass takes about 5 to 7 days to sprout. A full head of hair takes a few weeks to grow. The children really enjoy giving their grass heads haircuts!

Songs and Chants

BUBBLEGUM, BUBBLEGUM

Bubblegum, bubblegum in a dish.
How many pieces do you wish?
One, two, three…

If you like, you can replace the second line with "Tell me what choice do you wish?" for circle time activity choice or "Tell me which food do you wish?" for lunchtime.

ENGINE, ENGINE NUMBER NINE

Engine, engine number nine
Going down the Chicago line.
If the train goes off the track,
Do you want your money back?

TWINKLE, TWINKLE, LITTLE STAR

Twinkle, twinkle, little star,
How I wonder what you are!
Up above the world so high,
Like a diamond in the sky!
Twinkle, twinkle, little star,
How I wonder what you are!

HEAD, SHOULDERS, KNEES, AND TOES

Head, shoulders, knees, and toes, knees and toes
Head, shoulders, knees, and toes, knees and toes
And eyes and ears and mouth and nose
Head, shoulders, knees and toes, knees and toes!
(Repeat, getting faster each time.)

OPEN, SHUT THEM

(On "open," open both hands out wide in front of you, with palms facing away. On "shut them," close your hands into fists.)
Open, shut them, open, shut them,
Give a little clap, clap, clap. *(Clap three times.)*
Open, shut them, open, shut them,
Put them in your lap. *(Fold hands and put them in your lap.)*
Creep them, creep them,
Slowly creep them, *(Starting at the tummy, slowly "creep" fingers up toward the face.)*
Right up to your chin. *(Gently pull chin downward.)*
Open up your mouth. *(Open up your mouth.)*
But do not let them in! *(Pull hands behind your back.)*

THE WHEELS ON THE BUS

The wheels on the bus go round and round,
Round and round, round and round.
The wheels on the bus go round and round,
All through the town!

(Can continue with more lines.)
The people on the bus go up and down…
The driver on the bus says move on back…
The babies on the bus cry whaa whaa whaa…
The parents on the bus go shhh shhh shhh…
The horn on the bus goes beep beep beep…
The wipers on the bus go swish swish swish…
The lights on the bus go blink blink blink…
The doors on the bus go open and closed…

OLD MACDONALD HAD A FARM

Old MacDonald had a farm, E-I-E-I-O.
And on that farm he had a cow, E-I-E-I-O.
With a "moo, moo" here and a "moo, moo" there.
Here a "moo," there a "moo," everywhere a "moo, moo."
Old MacDonald had a farm, E-I-E-I-O.

Old MacDonald had a farm, E-I-E-I-O.
And on that farm he had a horse, E-I-E-I-O.
With a "neigh, neigh" here, and a "neigh, neigh" there.
Here a "neigh," there a "neigh," everywhere a "neigh, neigh."
Old MacDonald had a farm, E-I-E-I-O.
(Continue with other animals: dog, "woof, woof"; cat, "meow, meow"; pig, "oink, oink.")

WHERE IS THUMBKIN?

Where is Thumbkin? Where is Thumbkin?
Here I am! Here I am!
How are you today, sir? Very well, I thank you.
Run away. Run away.

Where is Pointer? Where is Pointer?
Here I am! Here I am!
How are you today, sir? Very well, I thank you.
Run away. Run away.

Where is Middleman? Where is Middleman? *(or Tall man)*
Here I am! Here I am!
How are you today, sir? Very well, I thank you.
Run away. Run away.

Where is Ring man? Where is Ring man?
Here I am! Here I am!
How are you today, sir? Very well, I thank you.
Run away. Run away.

Where is Pinkie? Where is Pinkie?
Here I am! Here I am!
How are you today, sir? Very well, I thank you.
Run away. Run away.

THE ITSY-BITSY SPIDER

The itsy-bitsy spider climbed up the water spout.
Down came the rain, and washed the spider out.
Out came the sun and dried up all the rain,
And the itsy-bitsy spider climbed up the spout again.

MAKE NEW FRIENDS BUT KEEP THE OLD

Make new friends, but keep the old.
One is silver, and the other is gold.
A circle's round; it has no end.
That's how long I want to be your friend.

THE MORE WE GET TOGETHER

The more we get together, together, together,
The more we get together, the happier we'll be,
'Cause your friends are my friends,
And my friends are your friends!
The more we get together, the happier we'll be!
(Can add other lines: "play together," "dance together.")

TOMMY THUMB

Tommy Thumb is up, and Tommy Thumb is down.
Tommy Thumb is dancing all around the town.
Dance him on your shoulders, dance him on your head,
Dance him on your knees then tuck him into bed.

THIS LITTLE PIGGY

This little piggy went to market.
This little piggy stayed home.
This little piggy had roast beef.
This little piggy had none.
And this little piggy cried,
"Wee-wee-wee!" all the way home.

WHO ARE THE PEOPLE IN YOUR FAMILY?

(Tune: "Who Are the People in Your Neighborhood?")
Oh, who are the people in your family, in your
family, in your family?
Oh, who are the people in your family?
They're the people that you love each day!

KISS THE BABY GOOD NIGHT

Now it's time to go to sleep.
Put the baby in the bed.
Cover the baby with the blanket,
And kiss the baby good night!
(Say "Whaaaaa whaaaa," like a crying baby.)
What does the baby need?
Give the baby a bottle.
(Repeat again with different answers.)
Give the baby a diaper change.
Give the baby a pacifier, and so on.

ROCK-A-BYE, BABY

Rock-a-bye, baby, in the treetop.
When the wind blows,
The cradle will rock.
When the bough breaks,
The cradle will fall,
And _____ will catch you cradle and all!
*(Child chooses who will catch the baby: Mommy,
Daddy, and so on.)*

GOOD NIGHT, BABIES

(Tune: "Good Night, Ladies")
Good night, babies, *(Have children lie on floor and
pretend to sleep.)*
Good night, babies, *(Begin to let voice get softer.)*
Good night, babies, it's time to go to sleep!
(Repeat until a quiet whisper.)
Wake up babies, *(Sing louder, and clap hands for
children to get up and jump or dance.)*
Wake up, babies,
Wake up, babies, it's time to start your day!

DRIVE, DRIVE, DRIVE THE TRUCK

(Tune: "Row, Row, Row Your Boat")
Drive, drive, drive the truck,
Carefully down the road.
Bumpity, bumpity, bumpity, bump.
Listen to my horn—BEEP BEEP!

DO YOU KNOW WHAT TOOL THIS IS?

(Tune: "The Muffin Man?)
Oh do you know what tool this is, what tool this is,
what tool this is?
Do you know what tool this is I'm holding in my
hand?
*(Hold up one tool at a time for children to guess, for
example, "A saw!")*

THIS IS THE WAY WE USE OUR TOOLS

(Tune: "Here We Go 'Round the Mulberry Bush")
This is the way we hammer the nails, hammer the
nails, hammer the nails.
This is the way we hammer the nails so early in
the morning.
This is the way we turn the screw, turn the screw,
turn the screw.
This is the way we turn the screw so early in the
morning.
*(Can continue with other construction items: saw,
paint, bricks, and so on.)*

WAY UP HIGH IN THE APPLE TREE

Way up high in the apple tree, *(Hold arms over
head.)*
Two little apples smiled at me. *(Use fingers to make
smile on face.)*
I shook that tree as hard as I could. *(Pretend to
shake tree.)*
Down fell the apples. *(Make fists and drop them to
ground.)*
Mmmmm, were they good! *(Smile and rub stomach.)*

I'M A LITTLE CHICKIE

(Tune: "I'm a Little Teapot")
I'm a little chickie, ready to hatch!
Pecking at my shell—scratch, scratch, scratch!
When I crack it open, out I'll leap!
Fluff my feathers—cheep, cheep, cheep.

I WANNA BE A BUTTERFLY

I wanna be a butterfly, a butterfly, a butterfly.
I wanna be a butterfly, just for fun!
First I'll be an egg, an egg, an egg.
First I'll be an egg, just for fun!
Then I'll be a caterpillar, caterpillar, caterpillar.
Then I'll be a caterpillar, just for fun!
Next I'll be a chrysalis, a chrysalis, a chrysalis.
Next I'll be a chrysalis, just for fun!
Now I am a butterfly, a butterfly, a butterfly.
Now I am a butterfly, just for fun!

CATERPILLAR, CATERPILLAR

Caterpillar, caterpillar—crawl, crawl, crawl,
Crawling on the ground, crawling all around.
Crawl, crawl, crawl!

THERE WAS A LITTLE TURTLE

There was a little turtle
That lived in a box. *(Put your hands together to make a box.)*
He swam in a puddle, *(Make swimming movements.)*
And he climbed on the rocks.
He snapped at a mosquito. *(Snap your fingers.)*
He snapped at a flea. *(Snap your fingers.)*
He snapped at a minnow, *(Snap your fingers.)*
And he snapped at me. *(Snap your fingers.)*
He caught the mosquito. *(Clap your hands.)*
He caught the flea. *(Clap your hands.)*
He caught the minnow, *(Clap your hands.)*
But he didn't catch me! *(Point your thumb at self and smile.)*

DO YOU KNOW WHAT COLOR THIS IS?

(Tune: "The Muffin Man")
Oh do you know what color this is, what color this is, what color this is?
Do you know what color this is I'm holding in my hand?
(Hold up one color at a time for children to guess, for example, "Green!")

I WANNA BE A FROG

I wanna be a frog, a frog, a frog.
I wanna be a frog, just for fun!
First I'll be an egg, an egg, an egg.
First I'll be an egg, just for fun!
Then I'll be a tadpole, a tadpole, a tadpole.
Then I'll be a tadpole, just for fun!
Next I'll be a froglet, a froglet, a froglet.
Next I'll be a froglet, just for fun!
Now I am a frog, a frog, a frog.
Now I am a frog, just for fun!

WE'RE GOING TO KENTUCKY

We're going to Kentucky, we're going to the fair
To see the senorita with flowers in her hair.
Shake it baby, shake it.
Shake it if you can.
Shake it like a milkshake,
And shake it again. Wahoo!

FIVE LITTLE DUCKS

Five little ducks went out one day
Over the hills and far away.
Mother duck said, "Quack, quack, quack, quack,"
But only four little ducks came waddling back.

Four little ducks went out one day
Over the hills and far away.
Mother duck said, "Quack, quack, quack, quack,"
But only three little ducks came waddling back.

Three little ducks went out one day
Over the hills and far away.

Mother duck said, "Quack, quack, quack, quack,"
But only two little ducks came waddling back.

Two little ducks went out one day
Over the hills and far away.
Mother duck said, "Quack, quack, quack, quack,"
But only one little duck came waddling back.

One little duck went out one day
Over the hills and far away.
Mother duck said, "Quack, quack, quack, quack,"
But no little ducks came waddling back.

Sad mother duck went out one day
Over the hills and far away.
Mother duck said, "Quack, quack, quack, quack,"
And all five ducks came waddling back!

FIVE GREEN AND SPECKLED FROGS

Five green and speckled frogs sat on a
    speckled log,
Eating the most delicious bugs. Yum, yum!
One jumped into the pool, where it was nice
    and cool,
Now there are four green speckled frogs.
    Glub, glub!

Four green and speckled frogs sat on a
    speckled log,
Eating the most delicious bugs. Yum, yum!
One jumped into the pool, where it was nice
    and cool,
Now there are three green speckled frogs.
    Glub, glub!
(Continue counting down: Three… Two…)

One green and speckled frog sat on a
    speckled log,
He jumped into the pool, where it was nice
    and cool,
Now there are no green speckled frogs.
    Glub, glub!

GRAY SQUIRREL

Gray squirrel, gray squirrel,
Swish your bushy tail. *(Wiggle tail.)*

Gray squirrel, gray squirrel,
Swish your bushy tail. *(Wiggle tail.)*
Wrinkle up your funny nose, *(Wrinkle nose.)*
Hold a nut between your toes. *(Pretend to hold a
    nut; or make paper/laminated acorns to hold.)*
Gray squirrel, gray squirrel,
Swish your bushy tail.

AUTUMN LEAVES ARE FALLING DOWN

(Tune: "London Bridge")
Autumn leaves are falling down, falling down,
    falling down.
Autumn leaves are falling down. Red, yellow,
    brown!
*(Stand holding arms up high with fingers wiggling
    like the leaves falling down. Begin to crouch
    down to floor.)*

Rake them up and make a pile, make a pile, make
    a pile.
Rake them up and make a pile. Red, yellow,
    brown!
(Pretend to rake leaves.)

LOVE, LOVE, LOVE YOUR PETS

(Tune: "Row, Row, Row Your Boat")
Love, love, love your pets,
Love them every day,
Give them food, and water too,
Then let them run and play!

THE BEAR WENT OVER THE MOUNTAIN

The bear went over the mountain,
The bear went over the mountain,
The bear went over the mountain,
To see what he could see.
But all that he could see,
But all that he could see,
Was the other side of the mountain,
The other side of the mountain,
The other side of the mountain was all that he
    could see!

ON TOP OF SPAGHETTI

On top of spaghetti all covered with cheese,
I lost my poor meatball when somebody sneezed.
It rolled off the table and onto the floor,
And then my poor meatball rolled out of the door.
It rolled in the garden and under a bush,
And then my poor meatball was nothing but
    mush!

PEANUT BUTTER AND JELLY

First you take the peanuts and you crunch 'em,
    you crunch 'em,
First you take the peanuts and you crunch 'em,
    you crunch 'em,
For your peanut, peanut butter and jelly, peanut,
    peanut butter and jelly.

Then you take the grapes and you squish 'em,
    you squish 'em,
Then you take the grapes and you squish 'em,
    you squish 'em,
For your peanut, peanut butter and jelly, peanut,
    peanut butter and jelly.

Then you take the bread and you spread it,
    you spread it,
Then you take the bread and you spread it,
    you spread it,
For your peanut, peanut butter and jelly, peanut,
    peanut butter and jelly.

Then you take your sandwich and you eat it,
    you eat it!
Then you take your sandwich and you eat it,
    you eat it!
'Cause it's good peanut butter and jelly, good
    peanut butter and jelly!

First you take the peanuts and you crunch 'em,
Then you take the grapes and you squish 'em,
Then you take the bread and you spread it,
Then you take your sandwich and you eat it,
'Cause it's good peanut butter and jelly, good
    peanut butter and jelly!

LET'S GO TO THE GROCERY STORE

(Tune: "Mary Had a Little Lamb")
Let's go to the grocery store,
The grocery store, the grocery store.
Let's go to the grocery store
So we can buy some "grapes!"
*(Let children each take a turn at choosing a food
    to buy.)*

PATTY CAKE

Patty cake, patty cake, baker's man,
Bake me a cake as fast as you can.
Roll the dough and mark it with B,
And put it in the oven for baby and me.

THE MUFFIN MAN

Oh, do you know the muffin man,
The muffin man, the muffin man?
Oh, do you know the muffin man,
Who lives on Drury Lane?
Oh, yes, I know the muffin man,
The muffin man, the muffin man.
Oh, yes, I know the muffin man,
Who lives on Drury Lane.

I WISH I WERE A LITTLE HUNK OF MUD

Oh, I wish I were a little hunk of mud.
Oh, I wish I were a little hunk of mud.
Then I'd ooey and I'd gooey,
Under everybody's shoey.
Oh, I wish I were a little hunk of mud.

THREE LITTLE KITTENS

Three little kittens, they lost their mittens,
And they began to cry,
Oh, mother dear, we sadly fear,
Our mittens we have lost.
What! Lost your mittens,
You careless little kittens,
Then you shall have no pie.
Meow, meow, then you shall have no pie.

The three little kittens, they found their mittens,
And they began to cry,
Oh, mother dear, see here, see here,
Our mittens we have found.
What! Found your mittens,
You good little kittens,
Then you shall have some pie.
Purr-rr, purr-rr, then you shall have some pie.

Three little kittens, put on their mittens,
And soon ate up the pie.
Oh, mother dear, we sadly fear,
Our mittens we have soiled.
What! Soiled your mittens,
You careless little kittens,
And they began to sigh.
Meow, meow, and they began to sigh.

The three little kittens, they washed their mittens,
And hung them out to dry.
Oh, mother dear, see here, see here,
Our mittens we have washed!
What! Washed your mittens?
You darling little kittens!
But I smell a rat close by.
Meow, meow, we smell a rat close by.

FIVE LITTLE SNOWFLAKES

Five little snowflakes dancing all around, dancing
    all around, dancing all around,
Five little snowflakes dancing all around.
When the sun came out, one melted to the
    ground!
(Continue counting down: Four… Three… Two…
    One…)
No little snowflakes dancing all around, dancing
    all around, dancing all around,
No little snowflakes dancing all around.
When the sun came out, flowers popped up from
    the ground!

I'VE GOT TWO WARM MITTENS

(Tune: "He's Got the Whole World in His Hands")
I've got two warm mittens,
On my hands.
I've got two warm mittens,
On my hands.
I've got two warm mittens,
On my hands.
They keep me cozy on a winter's day!

THIS IS THE WAY WE PUT ON OUR MITTENS

(Tune: "Here We Go 'Round the Mulberry Bush")
This is the way we put on our mittens,
Put on our mittens, put on our mittens.
This is the way we put on our mittens so early in
    the morning!
(Can add in other clothes as well: boots, snow pants,
    and so on.)

WHERE, OH WHERE DID MY NEW MITTENS GO?

(Tune: "Where, Oh Where Has My Little Dog
    Gone?")
Oh where, oh where did my new mittens go?
Oh where, oh where can they be?
Oh, I have looked high and I have looked low.
Oh where, oh where can they be?

A CHUBBY LITTLE SNOWMAN

A chubby little snowman had a carrot nose.
Along came a bunny, and what do you suppose?
That hungry little bunny, looking for his lunch,
Ate that snowman's carrot nose,
Nibble, nibble, crunch!

RAIN, RAIN, GO AWAY

Rain, rain, go away.
Come again some other day.
We want to go outside and play.
Come again some other day.

SPRINGTIME RAIN

(Tune: "Twinkle, Twinkle, Little Star")
Sprinkle, sprinkle, springtime rain,
Tapping on my windowpane.
Raindrops falling to the ground,
Helping plants to grow all around.
Sprinkle, sprinkle, springtime rain,
Tapping on my windowpane.

IT'S RAINING, IT'S POURING

It's raining, it's pouring, the old man is snoring.
He went to bed and bumped his head
And couldn't get up in the morning.

DOWN BY THE STATION

Down by the station early in the morning,
See the little pufferbellies all in a row.
See the stationmaster turn the little handle.
Puff, puff, toot, toot—off we go!

WHAT SHAPE IS THIS?

(Tune: "The Muffin Man")
Do you know what shape this is?
What shape this is, what shape this is?
Do you know what shape this is,
I'm holding in my hand?
(Hold different shapes for the children to guess.)

MISTER SUN

Oh Mister Sun, Sun, Mister Golden Sun,
Please shine down on me.
Oh Mister Sun, Sun, Mister Golden Sun,
Hiding behind a tree.
These little children are asking you
To please come out so we can play with you.
Oh Mister Sun, Sun, Mister Golden Sun,
Please shine down on me.
Please shine down on me!

FIVE LITTLE FISHIES SWIMMING IN THE SEA

Five little fishies swimming in the sea,
Teasing Mr. Shark, "You can't catch me! You can't
catch me!"
Along came Mr. Shark as quiet as can be
And *snapped* that fishy right out of the sea!

DID YOU EVER SEE A FISHY?

(Tune: "Did You Ever See a Lassie?")
Did you ever see a fishy, a fishy, a fishy?
Did you ever see a fishy swim this way and that?
Swim this way and that way, and this way and that
way?
Did you ever see a fishy swim this way and that?

THE SEASHORE SONG

(Tune: "Do Your Ears Hang Low?")
Feel the sand in my toes,
Smell the ocean with my nose,
See the children splash and play
On a hot summer day.
Hear the ocean waves go *roar*
As they crash into the shore.
Taste the salty sea!

Index